THE NEW BASIS FOR EDUCATION[16]

I Can There Be a New Basis?

Can there be a new basis for education? Does the foundation upon which education rests really change? Is the educational system of one age necessarily unfitted to provide for the educational needs of the next? These, and a multitude of the similar questions which people interested in educational progress are asking themselves, arise out of the process of transition that is seemingly one of the fundamental propositions of the universe. All things change, and are changing, from the smallest cell to the most highly organized creature, the noblest mountain range, and the vastest sun in the heavens. To-day differs from yesterday as to-morrow must differ from to-day. All things are becoming.

Test this statement with the observed facts of life. Here is a garden, well-planted and watered. The soil is loamy and black. On all its surface there is nothing, save a clod here and there, to relieve the warm, moist regularity. Come to-morrow and the level surface is broken by tiny green shoots which have appeared at intervals, thrusting through the top crust. Next week the black earth is striped with rows of green. Onions, beets, lettuce, and peas are coming up. Go back to the hills which you climbed in boyhood, ascend their chasmed sides and note how even they have changed. Each year some part of them has disappeared into the rapid torrent. Had you been there in April, you might have seen particles of your beloved hills in every water-course, hurrying toward the lowlands and the sea. While you watch them, the clouds change in the sky, the sunset wanes, and the forest covers the bared hills. Nature, fickle mistress of our destinies, spreads a never-ending panorama before our eyes that we may recognize the one great law of her being,—the law of progression.

II Social Change

How well does this principle of change apply to the organization of society! The absolute monarchy of one age yields to the semi-democracy of the next. Yesterday the church itself traded in men's bodies,—holding slaves, and accepting, without question, the proceeds of slavery. To-day machines replace men in a thousand industries. To-morrow slavery is called into question, until in the dim-glowering nineteenth century, men will struggle and die by tens of thousands;—on the one side, those who believe that the man should be the slave; on the other, those who hold that the slavery of the machine is alone necessary and just. Thus is every social institution altered from age to age. Thus is effected that transformation which men have chosen to call progress.

How profoundly does this truth apply to the raw material of education,—the children who enroll in the schools! Under your very eyes they lose their childish ways, feel their steps along the precipice of adolescence, enter the wonderland of imagery and idealism, and pass on into the maturity of life. How vain is our hope that the child may remain a child; how worthless our prayer that adult life shall never lay her heavy burden of cares and responsibilities upon his beloved shoulders. Even while you raise your hands in supplication, the child has passed from your life forever, leaving naught save a man to confront you.

From these mighty scythe strokes which change sweeps across the meadows of time, naught is exempt. The petals fall from the fairest flower; the bluest sky becomes overcast; the greatest feats of history are surpassed; and the social machinery, adequate for the needs of one age, sinks into the insignificance of desuetude in the age which follows. Thus does the inevitable come to pass. Thus does the social institution, wrought through centuries of turmoil and anguish, become useless in the newer civilization which is arising on every hand. The educational system in its inception was well founded, but the changes of time invalidate the original idea. Yesterday the school fulfilled the needs of men. To-day it fails to meet a situation which reshapes itself with each rising and each setting of the sun.

Each epoch must have its institutions. With the work of the past as a background, the present must constantly reshape the institutions which the past has bequeathed to it. These modified institutions, handed on in turn by the present, must again be rebuilt to meet the needs of the future; and so on through each succeeding age.

III Keeping Up with the Times

At times the march of progress is so rapid that even the most advanced grow breathless with attempts to keep abreast of the vanguard. Again, marking time for ages, progressive movements seem wholly dead, and the path to the future is overgrown with tradition, and blocked by oblivion and decay. The rapid advances of the nineteenth century, challenging the quickest to keep pace, forced upon many institutions surroundings wholly foreign to their bent and scope.

Nowhere is this more true than in the case of the educational system, which had its rise in an age of individualized industry and governmental non-interference, and now faces a newly inaugurated socialization of industry and an impromptu system of government control.

The new basis of education lies in the changes which the nineteenth century wrought in industry, transforming village life into city dwelling, and substituting for the skilled mechanic, using a tool, the machine, employing the unskilled worker. The men of the eighteenth century made political institutions, and were content with democracy; the men of the nineteenth century, accepting government as it stood, built up a new industry. The society which we in the twentieth century must erect upon the political and industrial triumphs of our forefathers, can never be successful unless it recognizes the fundamental character of the issues which nineteenth century industry and eighteenth century politics have brought into twentieth century life.

Is it too much to ask that the school stand foremost in this recognition of change, when it is in the school that the ideas of the new generation are moulded, tempered, and burnished? May we not expect that in its lessons to the young our educational system shall speak the language of the twentieth century rather than that of the eighteenth?

IV Education in the Early Home

Before the modern system of industry had its inception, while the old hand trades still held sway, at a time when the household was the center of work and pleasure, when the family made its butter, cheese, oatmeal, ale, clothing, tools, and utensils,—in such an atmosphere of domestic industry, Froebel wrote his famous "Education of Man." Note this description of the way in which a father may educate his son. "The son accompanies his father everywhere, to the field and to the garden, to the shop and to the counting house, to the forest and to the meadow; in the care of domestic animals and in the making of small articles of household furniture; in the splitting, sawing, and piling up of wood; in all the work his father's trade or calling involves."[17] In another passage he calls upon parents, "more particularly fathers (for to their special care and guidance the child ripening into boyhood is confided)," to contemplate "their parental duties in child guidance;"[18] and he prefaces this exhortation with a long list of illustrations, suggesting the methods which may be pursued by the farm laborer, the goose-herd, the gardener, the forester, the blacksmith, and other tradesmen and craftsmen, in the education of their sons. Any such man, Froebel points out, may take his child at the age of two or three and teach him some of the simple rules of his trade. How different is the position of the son of a workman in a modern American city! An American city dweller reading Froebel's discussion would not conceive of it as applying in any sense to him, or to his life.

V City Life and the New Basis for Education

The very thought of city life precludes the possibility of home work. The narrow house, the tenement, the great shop or factory, on the one hand, prevent the mechanic from carrying on his trade near his family; and on the other hand, make it impossible for the father whose work lies far from his home to give his boys the "special care and guidance" about which Froebel writes.

The system of industry which was established in England during the closing decades of the eighteenth century, and which secured a foothold in both Germany and the United States during the first half of the nineteenth century, has revolutionized the basis of our lives. The workshop has been transplanted from the home to the factory; both men and women leave their homes for ten, eleven, or even twelve hours a day to carry on their industrial activities; great centers of population collect about the centers of industry; the farm, the flock of geese, the garden, the forest, and the blacksmith shop disappear; food, clothing, and other necessaries of life—formerly the product of home industry—are produced in great factories; and the city home, stripped of its industrial functions, restricted in scope, robbed of its adults, presents little opportunity for the education of the city child. Standing on the threshold of his meager dwelling, this child of six looks forward to a life which must be based on the instruction provided in a public school system.

The country boy still has his ten-acre lot, where he may run and play. There are flowers and freckles in the spring; kite-flying, fishing, hunting, and trapping in summer and autumn. The general farm is a storehouse of useful information in rudimentary form. From day to day and from year to year the country boy may learn and enjoy.

The city boy is differently situated. His playground is the street, where he plays under the wheels of wagons, automobiles, and trolley cars; or else he plays in a public playground in company with hundreds, or even thousands, of other children. Even then his activities are restricted by city ordinances, monitors, policemen, and other exponents of law and order.

The city home, whether tenement or single house, cannot begin to supply the opportunities for growth and development which were furnished by life in the open. Where else, then, does the responsibility for such growth and development rest than upon the school? On the farm the boy learned his trade, as Froebel suggests, at the hands of his father. The father of the city boy spends his working hours in a mill, or in an office, where boys under fourteen or sixteen are forbidden by law to go. The city home is unavoidably deprived of the chance to provide adequate recreation or adequate vocational training for its children. The burden in both cases shifts to the school.

A hundred years ago practically all industries were carried on in connection with the home. The weaver, the carpenter, the hatter, the cobbler, the miller, lived and worked on the same premises. Then steam was applied to industry; the machine replaced the man; semi-skilled and unskilled labor replaced skilled labor; great numbers of men and women, and even of children, crowded together in factories to spin thread, make bolts and washers, weave ribbon, bake bread, manufacture machinery, or do some one of the many hundreds of things now done in factories. The change from home industry to factory industry is well named the Industrial Revolution. It completely overturned the established and accepted means of making a living.

The industrial upheaval has changed every phase of modern life. Industry itself has replaced apprenticeship by a degree of specialization undreamed of in primitive life. From the superintendent to the office boy, from the boss roller to the yard laborer, from the chief clerk to the stenographer, the work of men and women is monotonous and specialized. The city has grown up as a logical product of an industrial system which centers thousands, or even tens of thousands, of workmen in one place of employment. The city home differs fundamentally from the country home as the city differs from the country.

The changes now going on in farming are no less significant than those which the nineteenth century witnessed in manufacturing. Science has been applied to agriculture. Old methods are brought into question. Intensive study and specialization are widespread. The time has passed when a farmer can afford to neglect the agricultural bulletins or papers. To be successful, he must be a trained specialist in his line, and the school and college are called upon to provide the training.

No individual is responsible for these changes. They have come as the logical product of a long series of discoveries and inventions. New methods, built upon the ideas and methods of the past, have created a new civilization.

The civilized world, reorganized and reconstituted, rebuilt in all of its economic phases, demands a new teaching which shall relate men and women to the changed conditions of life. This is the new basis for education,—this the new foundation upon which must be erected a superstructure of educational opportunity for succeeding generations. It remains for education to recognize the change and to remodel the institutions of education in such a way that they shall meet the new needs of the new life.

FOOTNOTES:

[16] Portions of this chapter originally appeared in The Journal of Education.

[17] "The Education of Man," F. Froebel. Translated by W. N. Halliman, New York; D. Appleton & Co. 1909, p. 103.

[18] Ibid., p. 187.

CHAPTER II

TEACHING BOYS AND GIRLS

I The New School Machinery

The influence which the industrial changes of the past hundred years has had on education is considerable. With the transformation of the home workshop into the factory has come the transition from rural and village life to life in great industrial cities and towns. The introduction of specialized machinery has placed upon education the burden of vocational training. More important still, it has so augmented the size of the educational problem that an intricate system of school machinery has been devised to keep the whole in order.

The rural, or village, school was a one or two-room affair, housing a handful of pupils. Aside from matters of discipline, the administration of the school was scarcely a problem. General superintendents, associate superintendents, compulsory attendance laws, card index systems, and purchasing departments were unknown. The school was a simple, personal business conducted by the teacher in very much the same way that the corner grocer conducted his store—on faith and memory.

The growth of cities and towns necessitated the introduction of elaborate school machinery. In place of a score of pupils, thousands, tens, and even hundreds of thousands were placed under the same general authority. City life made some form of administrative machinery inevitable.

The increasing size of the school system,—and in new, growing cities the school system increases with a rapidity equal to the rate of growth of the population,—leads to increase in class size. A school of twenty pupils is still common in rural districts. In the elementary grades of American city schools, investigators find fifty, sixty, and in some extreme cases, seventy pupils under the charge of one teacher, while the average number, per teacher, is about forty.

Recrimination is idle. The obvious fact remains that the rate of growth in school population is greater than the rate of growth in the school plant. The schools in many cities have not caught up with their educational problem. The result is a multiplication of administrative problems, not the least of which is the question of class size.

II Rousseau Versus a Class of Forty

A toilsome journey it is from the education of an individual child by an individual teacher (Rousseau's Emile) to the education of forty children by one teacher (the normal class in American elementary city schools). Rousseau pictured an ideal; we face a reality—complex, expanding, at times almost menacing.

The difference between Rousseau's ideal and the modern actuality is more serious than it appears superficially. Rousseau's idea permitted the teacher to treat the child as an individuality, studying the traits and peculiarities of the pupil, building up where weakness appeared, and directing freakish notions and ideas into conventional channels. The modern city school with one teacher and forty pupils places before the teacher a constant temptation, which at times reaches the proportions of an overmastering necessity, to treat the group of children as if each child were like all the rest. A teacher who can individualize forty children, understand the peculiarities of each child, and teach in a way that will enable each of the children to benefit fully by her instruction, is indeed a master, perhaps it would be fairer to say a super-master in pedagogy. A class of forty is almost inevitably taught as a group.

There is another feature about the large school system which is even more disastrous to the welfare of the individual child. Rousseau studied the individual to be educated, and then prescribed the course of study. The city teacher, no matter how intimately she may be acquainted with the needs of her children, has little or no say in deciding upon the subjects which she is to teach her class. Such matters are for the most part determined by a group of officials—principals, superintendents, and boards of education,—all of whom are engaged primarily in administrative work, and some of whom have never taught at all, nor entered a psychological laboratory, nor engaged in any other occupation that would give first-hand, practical, or theoretical knowledge of the problems encountered in determining a course of study.

A course of study must be devised, however, even though some of the responsible parties have no first-hand knowledge of the points at issue. The method by which it is devised is of peculiar importance to this discussion. The administrative officials, having in mind an average child, prepare a course of study which will meet that average child's needs. Theoretically, the plan is admirable. It suffers from one practical defect,—there is no such thing as an average child.

III The Fallacious "Average"

Averages are peculiarly tempting to Americans. They supply the same deeply-felt want in statistics that headlines do in newspapers. They tell the story at a glance. In this peculiar case the story is necessarily false.

An average may be taken only of like things. It is possible to average the figures 3, 4, and 8 by adding them together and dividing by 3. The average is 5. Such a process is mathematically correct, because all of the units comprising the 3, 4, and 8 are exactly alike. One of the premises of mathematics is that all units are alike, hence they may be averaged.

Unlike mathematical units, all children are different. They differ in physical, in mental, and in spiritual qualities. Their hair is different in color and in texture. Their feet and hands vary in size. Some children are apt at mathematics, others at drawing, and still others at both subjects. Some children have a strong sense of moral obligation,—an active conscience,—others have little or no moral stamina. No two children in a family are alike, and no two children in a school-room are alike. After an elaborate computation of hereditary possibilities, biologists announce that the chance of any two human creatures being exactly alike is one in five septillions. In simple English, it is quite remote.

IV The Five Ages of Childhood

A very ingenious statement of the case is made by Dr. Bird T. Baldwin. Children, says Dr. Baldwin, have five ages,—

1. A chronological age,
2. A physical age,
3. A mental age,
4. A moral age,
5. A school age.

Two children, born on the same day, have the same age in years. One is bound to grow faster than the other in some physical respect. Therefore the two children have different physical ages, or rates of development. In the same way they have differing mental and moral ages. The school age, a resultant of the first three, is a record of progress in school. Even when children are born on the same day, the chances that they will grow physically, mentally, and morally at exactly the same rate, and will make exactly the same progress in school, are remote indeed. School children are, therefore, inevitably different.

V Age Distribution in One Grade

A very effective illustration of the differences in chronological age, in school age, and in the rate of progress in school is furnished in the 1911 report of the superintendent of schools for Springfield, Mass. There are in this report a series of figures dealing with the ages, and time in school, of fifth-grade pupils in Springfield. The first table shows the number of years in school and the age of all the fifth-grade pupils.

TABLE 1

Age and Time in School, Fifth Grade, Springfield, December ,1911

Years in School	\multicolumn{13}{c}{Ages}	Total
	5	6	7	8	9	10	11	12	13	14	15	16	17	18	
1	..	..	..	..	..	..	1	..	..	..	..	..	..	..	1
2	..	..	..	2	1	1	1	2	2	..	..	..	..	..	9
3	..	..	..	6	38	25	9	..	1	1	..	..	..	..	80

4	..	..	..	..	162	200	63	12	10	3	..	..	..	..	450
5	..	..	..	..	17	178	131	47	14	2	..	..	..	..	389
6	..	..	..	..	1	11	120	60	29	3	..	..	..	..	224
7	..	..	..	..	..	1	3	46	29	8	1	..	1	..	88
8	..	..	..	..	..	..	1	4	17	4	1	..	..	..	28
9	..	..	..	..	..	..	..	..	..	4	1	..	..	..	5
10	..	..	..	..	..	..	..	..	..	1	..	..	..	..	1
11	..	..	..	..	..	..	..	..	..	..	..	..	..	..	
12	..	..	..	..	..	..	..	..	..	..	..	..	..	..	
13	..	..	..	..	..	..	..	..	..	..	..	..	..	..	
Total	..	..	..	8	219	416	329	171	102	26	3	..	1	..	1,275

Theoretically, children in Springfield enter the school at six, and spend one year in each grade. If all of the children in the Springfield schools had lived up to this theory, there would be 1,275 eleven years of age, and 1,275 in the fifth grade. A glance at the table shows that only 131, or about 10 per cent of the children, are both eleven years of age and five years in the school. Among the 1,275 fifth-grade children, 389, or 31 per cent, have been in school five years, and 329, or 26 per cent, are eleven years of age.

The superintendent follows this general table with other tables giving a more detailed analysis of over and under age pupils, and of rate of progress in school.

TABLE 2

Age and Progress Groups of Fifth-Grade Pupils in Springfield, December, 1911

	Young		Normal		Over-age		Total	
	No.	Per Cent	No.	Per Cent	No.	Per Cent	No.	Per Cent
Rapid	435	34	74	6	31	2	540	42
Normal	195	16	131	10	63	5	389	31
Slow	13	1	124	10	209	16	346	27

| | Total | 643 | 51 | 329 | 26 | 303 | 23 | 1,275 | 100 |

The inferences from Table 2 are very clear. Of the 1,275 fifth-grade pupils, 435, or 34 per cent, are not only under-age for the grade, but they have progressed at more than normal speed. They are the exceptionally capable pupils of the grade. At the other extreme we find 209 children, or 16 per cent of all in the grade, who need special attention because they are both over-age and slow. Feeble-minded children rarely advance beyond the second grade; hence we know that none of these are feeble-minded, but among their number will be found many who will be little profited by the ordinary curriculum; 110 of them are already 12 years old, and 75 are 13 years old. A majority of them will, in all probability, drop out of school as soon as they reach the age of 14, unless prior to that time some new element of interest is introduced that will make a strong appeal; for example, some activity toward a vocation.

A further study of the over-age column shows that 31 pupils, 2 per cent, are over-age, but they have reached their present position in less than usual time; while 63 of them, also over-age, have required the full five years to reach their present grade position. Unless by limiting the required work of these over-age pupils to the essentials, or by some administrative arrangement involving special grouping with relatively small numbers in a class, so that we can in the one case maintain, and in the other case bring about, accelerated progress, there is little likelihood that any large number will remain in school to complete the ninth grade, much less take a high school course; for four years hence their ages will range from 16 to 18 years. The 124 pupils who are of normal age, but slow, are also subjects for special attention, for they have repeated from one to three grades, or have failed to secure from two to six half-yearly promotions, and are in danger of acquiring the fatal habit of failure, if they have not already acquired it.

The superintendent then goes on to emphasize the imperative duty resting on each principal, to examine and to understand the varying capacities of individual children in his school. Without such an understanding real educational progress cannot be made.

This study is most illuminating. Nothing could more effectually show variation in individual children than the difference in one city grade of the most obvious of characteristics—age and progress in school. The infinitely greater variations in the subtle characteristics that distinguish children can be more readily guessed at than measured. Under these circumstances, the attempt to prepare studies for an "average child" is manifestly futile. The course may be organized, but it will hardly meet the needs of large numbers of the individual children who take it.

VI Shall Child or Subject Matter Come First?

The old education presupposed an average child, and then prepared a course of study which would fit his needs. The new education recognizes the absurdity of averaging unlike quantities, and accepts the ultimate truth that each child is an individual, differing in needs, capacity, outlook, energy, and enthusiasm from every other child. An arithmetic average can be struck, but when it is applied to children it is a hypothetical and not a real quantity. There is not, and never will be, an average child; hence, a school system planned to meet the needs of the average child fits the needs of no child at all.

Mathematics may be taught to the average child. So may history and geography. While subject matter comes first in the minds of educators, a course of study designed to meet average conditions is a possibility. The moment, however, that the schools cease to teach subjects and begin to teach boys and girls, such a proceeding is out of the question.

The temptation in a complex school system, where children are grouped by hundreds and thousands, to allow the detail of administration to overtop the functions of education is often irresistible. The teacher with forty pupils learns to look upon her pupils as units. The superintendent and principals, seeking ardently for an overburdened commercial ideal named "efficiency," sacrifice everything else to the perfection of the mechanism. Among the smooth clicking cogs, child individuality has only the barest chance for survival.

VII The Vicious Practices of One "Good" School

There are school systems in which organization has overgrown child welfare, in which pedagogy has usurped the place of teaching. In such systems the teacher teaches the prescribed course of study, whether or no. The officers of administration, aiming at some mechanical ideal, shape the schools to meet the requirements of system.

The proneness of some teachers and school administrators alike to overemphasize mechanics, and to underemphasize the welfare of individual children is well illustrated in a recent statement by Dr. W. E. Chancellor, who, in writing of a first-hand investigation made in a city in the Northeast, describes a condition which he says "I know by fairly authoritative reports does exist in a considerable number of cities and towns—not merely in a school here and there, but generally and characteristically.

"In the city to which I definitely refer," Dr. Chancellor continues, "I found that the intermediate and grammar grade teachers had systematically, deliberately, and successfully sacrificed hundreds of boys and girls upon the altar of examinations to the fetish of good schools. They have been so anxious to have good schools that they have kept an average of 20 per cent of their pupils one grade lower than they belong. In some schools the average runs to above 35 per cent.

"Some teachers and some school superintendents cannot see that the school is simply a machine for developing boys and girls; cannot see that the machine in itself is worthless save as it contributes to human welfare. A school may be so good as actually to damage the souls and bodies of human beings. It damages their souls when the machine operators, seeking 75 per cent in every subject, keep boys and girls in grammar schools until they average sixteen years of age."[19] Dr. Chancellor continues with a stinging arraignment of school officials who sacrifice children to systems.

The article strikes an answering chord in the experiences of many men and women. A friend came recently to our bungalow, and, with a troubled face, spoke of his daughter's ill-health.

"She is not sick," he said, "but just ailing. These first May days have taken her appetite. She needs the country air."

The daughter was a dear little girl of twelve—any one might have envied the father of his treasure—and we offered to keep her with us for a month in the country, and to go over her school work with her every day. The father accepted our proposal on the spot, but two days later he came back to say that he could not make the arrangements.

"It cannot be done," he explained, "because the school will not let her off. I told the principal about my daughter's health and showed him the advantage of a month in the country with her school work carefully supervised. Her school is rather crowded, and as I want her to go on with her class in the autumn, I asked him if he could arrange to keep her place for her. In reply he said,—

"'I cannot do as you wish. Such cases as yours interfere seriously with the working of the school.'"

VIII Boys and Girls—The One Object of Educational Activity

Perhaps our language was not as temperate as it should have been, but we told that father something which we would fain repeat until every educator and every parent in the United States has heard it and written it on the tables of his heart,—

THE ONE OBJECT OF EDUCATION IS TO ASSIST AND PREPARE CHILDREN TO LIVE.

Why have we established a billion-dollar school system in the United States? Is it to pay teachers' salaries, to build new school houses, and to print text-books by the million? Hardly. These things are incidents of school business, but they are no more reason for the school's existence than fertilizer and seed are reasons for making a garden. Gardens are cultivated in order to secure plants and flowers; the school organization of which Americans so often boast exists to educate children.

"Of course," you exclaim, "we knew that before." Did you? Then why was my friend forced to choose between the wreck of his daughter's health and the disarrangement of a bit of school machinery? Why is Dr. Chancellor able to describe a situation existing "generally and characteristically," in which the welfare of children is bartered away for high promotion averages? The truth is that society still tolerates, and often accepts, the belief that the purpose of education is the formation of a school system. We have yet to learn that, to use Herbert Spencer's phrase, the object of education is the preparation of children for complete living.

Education exists for the purpose of preparing and assisting children to live. To do that work effectively, it must devote only so much effort to school administration and to school machinery as will perform for boys and girls that very effective service.

No two children are alike, and no two children have exactly similar needs. There are, however, certain kinds of needs which all children have in common. It is obviously impossible to discuss in the abstract the needs of any individual child. It is just as obviously possible to analyze child needs, and to classify them in workable groups. It is true that all children are different; so are all roses different, yet all have petals and thorns in common. Similarly, there are certain needs which are common to all children who play, who grow, who live among their fellows, and who expect to do something in life. The matter may be stated more concretely thus,—

I. The school exists to assist and prepare children to live.

II. Living involves three kinds of needs, which it is the duty of the school to understand and interpret.

    1. Needs which the child has because he is a physical being.

    2. Needs which result from the child's surroundings.

    3. Needs which arise in connection with the things which the child hopes to do in life.

A further analysis of these groups of needs constitutes the subject matter of the next chapter.

FOOTNOTES:

[19] Sacrificing Children, W. E. Chancellor, Journal of Education, Vol. 77, pp. 564-565 (May 22, 1913).

CHAPTER III

FITTING SCHOOLS TO CHILDREN

I Child Growth—A Primary Factor in Child Life

In the first place children have certain needs because in common with many other living creatures they develop through spontaneous, self-expressive activity. The growth of children is a growth in body, in mind and in soul.

During the first six years of life the bodies of children grow rapidly, and during these years we wisely make no attempt to train their minds. From six to twelve or thirteen body growth is slower, the mind is having its turn at development, and during these years the children start to school.

Then, at twelve or thirteen or fourteen, differing with different races and different individuals, all normal children enter the fairyland of adolescence. Life takes on new meanings, human relationships are closer, great currents of feeling run deep and strong through the child's being, because there is coming into his life one of the most wonderful of human experiences—the dawning of sex consciousness.

This period of sex awakening produces a profound change in the lives of boys, but it works an even greater transformation in the lives of girls. For both sexes it is a time of rapid physical growth and of severe mental and spiritual strain. It is a time when the energies of the body are so entirely devoted to the development of sex functions that great mental stress should above all things be avoided, yet it is at this very time—think of it!—when we send our boys and girls to high school, and force them to spend a great part of their waking hours in severe intellectual efforts.

II Children Need Health First

Had we set out with the deliberate intention of torturing our children we could have devised no better method. If we had applied ourselves to physiology, found out the time when the child needed the most energy for physical growth and the most relief from mental strain, and had then set out to plan a course of study which would wreck his health, we should have built a school system which gave him the comparatively easy work of the elementary grades until he was fourteen, and then, at the most critical period of his life, sent him into a new system of schools to study new, abstract subjects.

What is it that our children must have before they can acquire anything else? Health! We cry the word aloud, emphasizing and exhorting—nothing without health! Yet, despite our protest, at a period of rapid physical growth, at the time of severe spiritual trial, there yawns the high school—grim for boys, ghastly for girls—with its ever-recurring demand: "Work, study; study, work."

Considering the child's physical welfare, the high school is placed at exactly the point (fourteen to eighteen years) where it is best calculated to destroy the delicate balance of sanity, rendering its victims unable to stand the burden and heat of life's later day.

We cannot escape the fact that children have bodies. The first duty of the schools, therefore, is to recognize the existence of these bodies by giving them due attention, particularly at the crucial periods of physical growth. Therefore every school must provide as much physical training as is necessary to insure normal body growth at each particular age.

Then there are certain rules of health—"hygiene," they are called—which should be taught to every child. Since bodies do not stay normal if they are abused every child should have right ideas of body care.

Most important of all, the schools must instruct children in sex hygiene because the growth of sex consciousness is one of the most significant of the changes which occur in the life of a child.

"But must sex hygiene be taught in the school?" you will ask.

Undoubtedly it must. If it were a choice between sex instruction in the home or in the school, there would be no hesitation about delegating it to the home; but since most homes neglect the discussion of sex matters, leaving the children to gain their knowledge of sex from unreliable sources on the streets, the choice lies between the perversion of sex as it is taught on the streets, and the science of sex as it should be taught in the schools.

III Play as a Means to Growth

Children's minds grow as well as their bodies—grow in retention, in grasp, and in power. Memory work (the learning of poems, songs, and formulas) helps to make minds more retentive, while all studies, but particularly number work, increase mental grasp and power.

Besides body growth and mind growth all children have soul growth. They develop human sympathy, and they are interested in esthetic things. To supply these needs the school must give the child literature and art. Simple these lessons must be, particularly in the elementary grades; but there is scarcely a child who will not respond to the noble in literature or the beautiful in art if these things are presented to him in an understandable way.

The bodies, minds, and souls of children grow. They are all sacred. Each child needs a normal body, an active mind, a healthy and a beautiful soul. We dare not develop bodies at the expense of minds and souls, but neither may we educate minds at the expense of souls and bodies—a tendency which has been fearfully prevalent in American education.

The most valuable means of securing this all-important growth is "play," which Froebel said contained the germinal leaves of all later life. Growth comes only through expression. One does not develop muscle by watching the strong man in the circus, but by exercising. The child's chief means of expression is through play, hence play is the child's method of securing growth.

In their earliest infancy children play. Their frolics and antics are really "puppy play," the product of overflowing life and animal spirits. At this "puppy play" stage, when the child plays merely to work off surplus energy, the most essential thing is a place to play, and the school must meet this need by providing playgrounds.

As children grow older they turn to a more advanced type of play. Instead of romping and frolicking individually they play in groups. It is in these group plays that the child gets his first idea of the duty which he owes to his fellows, his first glimmering of a social sense. In the home and in the school he is in a subordinate position, but in the "gang," or "set," he is as good as the next. Group play teaches democracy. More than that, group play has a moral value. Each one must play fair. Those who do not are ruthlessly ostracized, so children learn to abide by the decision of the crowd. While children's plays should be as untrammeled as possible, it is the duty of the school to stimulate group play by suggesting new games, organizing athletic meets, getting up interclass sports, and in other ways supervising and directing games and sports.

In the course of the child's life play takes another form, the form of creative work. Boys build wagons and houses; girls cook, and make dolls. The "puppy play" of their early childhood has evolved into a form of creative activity that sooner or later grips every human creature. We want to plant, to build, to plan, to make. It is the creative power within us yearning for expression, hence the well-planned school will provide simple forms of manual training by means of which both boys and girls will be taught to use their hands so skillfully that they may translate an idea into a concrete product.

Civilization has been described as the art of playing. Big folks are apt to look down on play because most of it is done by children. But listen, big folks: When Anna plays dolls she does it in a frank, serious, whole-souled way that you seldom imitate. There is no activity so vital to the child as play, nor does any man succeed at his work unless he can "play at it" with the fervor and abandon of a child.

IV Some Things Which a Child Must Learn

So much for the needs which a child has because he is a living creature. Suppose we turn now to some other needs—the needs which arise because the child is in a great universe and surrounded by his fellowmen. Wherever a child lives and whatever he does he must always face certain surrounding conditions. First among his surroundings are people. No one except Robinson Crusoe can get away from people, and even Crusoe had his man Friday.

Since we are compelled, whether we like it or not, to live with people, the school must teach language (oral and written), in order that the children may learn to tell others what they think, and may likewise understand the thoughts of others. The better the language the more clearly can they understand each other.

In order that children may have a proper respect for the rights of others the school should teach ethics by means of simple stories about people. Teachers should explain how men live in groups, and how, if group life is to be tolerable, men must respect each other's rights.

Perhaps in the upper elementary grades, and certainly in the high school, there should be some simple work in psychology in order that children may know how people's minds work.

Then besides the people of the present there are the people of the past, and, because the things which they did enable us to live as we do, children should be taught history, particularly the history of their own country, state, and town.

The child comes into contact, in addition to people, with the institutions which people have constructed—the home, the school, the state, the industrial system. Every child who grows to maturity will participate in the activity of these institutions, hence every child should be taught about them. In the last two years of the elementary grades civics can be successfully taught, since even at twelve years children are interested in the things which are happening around them. In the high schools this work can be carried much further in the form of social and industrial problem courses.

The most universal and by far the largest of the child's surroundings consist of the things about him. He lives in a world, a very little world to be sure, but to him it is great; and a knowledge of the world comes through a study of geography. Beginning with the geography of his native town (not with the basin of the Ganges) he can learn successively about the geography of the county, the state, the country, and then of the world.

Surrounding the child on every hand are plants and animals. Nature study gives him an intelligent interest in them. As he grows older general nature study may be subdivided into geology, botany, zoology; and the forces of nature may be examined in astronomy, chemistry, and physics: but most of these subjects are too specialized for the elementary grades, and should appear, if at all, in the high schools.

There is a group of courses which belongs in every school—elementary school as well as high school—namely, the courses which prepare children for life activity. Growth and training in the art of living enable children to fulfill the third function of their being—that of doing. Every man and every woman needs work in order to live, and it is a part of the duty of education to prepare them for that work.

First of all, as modern society has developed, every man and many women need an income-producing trade or occupation; hence it is the duty of the schools to provide trade and professional educations (really the same thing under different names). No child should be permitted to leave the schools until he is proficient in some income-giving work. The character of the teaching must be altered to suit the locality, but the principle is absolute.

Further, since men should not devote their entire lives to the same task, because they require a change of occupation, the school should aim to provide an avocation, or secondary occupation, which may occupy leisure hours. Manual training, agriculture, art work, and civics will supply different people with occupations for spare time.

Finally, since one of the chief duties of society is to insure a healthy and increasingly valuable supply of human beings, no one should leave the schools without a thorough domestic training, including training for parenthood. While this training should be given in a measure to boys, it should be intended primarily for girls, and should include biology, hygiene, chemistry, dietetics, psychology, and nursing. Although the elementary grades can provide only the simplest training along these lines that training should be given to every future housekeeper and mother.

V What Schools Must Provide to Meet Child Needs

If, up to this point, we have rightly described child needs, the school must be so organized as to provide for growth and play, for instructing the child in a knowledge of people, institutions, things and ideas, and for preparing every child to do his work in life.

These subjects must be so apportioned over the grades that each child has the benefit of them. The high school is a continuation of the elementary school. It is in the high school that children should begin to specialize, because specialization before the beginning of adolescence is undesirable; but since, in many localities, almost all of the children leave before reaching the high school, these subjects must be taught in the elementary grades. Certain things every child must know. If he is going to drop school at fourteen, as three-quarters of the American school children do, he must be reached in the first eight school grades. If he goes to high school he may there be given an opportunity to complete and intensify the education which the elementary school has started.

We believe that these fundamental principles of education are sufficiently flexible to fit any community in the United States; they will apply to places of the most divergent school needs.

VI The Educational Work of the Small Town

Let us begin by applying the scheme to a mining village of three thousand inhabitants, a typical industrial community.

In this village more than nine-tenths of the children leave school at or before fourteen years of age, so that whatever school training they get must be secured between the ages of six and fourteen.

The kind of activities that the children will take up in life is fixed by the custom of the town. The great majority of the boys go into the mines or shops, while practically all of the girls help around the home until they marry. A small number work in stores and factories.

The life is rather primitive; the houses are set far apart; the children have an abundance of play space; they are required to do chores in homes where they receive little home training. The town affords an unparalleled opportunity to learn nasty things in a nasty way.

Almost all of the educational work in such a town must be done in the elementary schools. While high school facilities may be afforded they will appeal to a vanishingly small percentage of the children.

The elementary schools in such a village must provide organized games for the younger children and organized sports for the older ones; a sufficient amount of physical training to insure robust bodies; careful instruction in physiology, body hygiene, and sex hygiene; simple manual training for the younger children; thorough preparation in the reading and writing of English; the fundamentals of numbers; geography with particular reference to the geographic conditions in the immediate locality; civics and history—particularly American history; a thorough drill in English and American literature; a minimum amount of instruction in fine art—drawing, painting, modeling; an extensive system of nature study, supplemented by field trips.

This course should be required of boys and girls alike. In addition to these studies the boys in a coal-mining village should receive careful instruction in geology, particularly in the mineralogy of the region in which the mine is located; technical training in mining, drafting, and shop work; and a sufficient training in agriculture to enable them to make good kitchen gardens, since gardening is one of the chief avocations of men in such a community.

Parallel to this special training for boys the schools should provide for girls a thorough course in domestic science, with particular emphasis on economical purchasing, and an education for parenthood, including hygiene, dietetics, psychology, and nursing.

Such a course of study given in a typical mining village would tend to make of the boys educated, trained workmen, and of the girls educated, trained mothers. To be sure this course would not make of the boys railroad presidents or United States senators; but even that is not a drawback because, incredible as it may sound to many old-fashioned ears, the vast majority of these boys will be miners and mechanics. The question is, therefore, Shall they be good miners or bad ones? United States senatorships bother them not a whit.

If there are, as there always will be in such a village, a few exceptional children who desire more advanced work, the teacher can do exactly what he does now—namely, give them special instruction.

Such an educational system as that outlined would require more training in the teachers, and an additional outlay for tools and school-rooms, but it would train the boys and girls of the village to live their lives effectively.

The mine-village educational problem is rendered especially easy of solution because the community is small in size, and because there are only two occupations, mining and homekeeping, into which the children go.

A similar situation may be found in most of the agricultural districts, except that the boys take up farming instead of mining, while the girls are called upon to participate in farm work to the extent of caring for chickens and pigs, and sometimes for milk. In such an agricultural community the same outline for study might apply, except that in training for occupations boys should be taught the facts regarding soil fertility, fruit culture, dairying, market gardening, and other agricultural problems, while girls need instruction which will fit them for domestic life and for parenthood.

In New York State a number of agricultural high schools giving a course such as the one just hinted at, have met with marked success. Most country children do not go to high school, however—although they are doing so in increasing numbers—and hence the necessity for shaping the elementary course along similar lines.

VII The Educational Problems of an Industrial Community

When the mining village and the farming district are replaced by the industrial town and the city, the school problem is greatly complicated by the crowding of many people into a small space and by the great diversity of occupations which the people pursue. The larger the town the worse the crowding and the greater the variety of jobs. Otherwise the problem of education remains largely the same.

The most apparent need of the town child is a place to play, and the plainest duty of the town elementary school is to provide play space. In thinly settled places there is no such need. In towns and cities there is no more imperative duty resting on the school than the furnishing of playgrounds and gymnasiums for children. The practice of building school houses without gymnasiums and without play spaces cannot be too strongly condemned. It is robbing children of the chance to grow into normal human beings.

The other side of the town problem—the question of occupations—has been settled in Germany, and more recently in certain American cities, by the "continuation" school, which unties the Gordian knot by cutting it. Instead of allowing children to stop school at fourteen the "continuation" system requires partial school attendance until they are eighteen.

Under this system, when children reach the end of the elementary schools they may either go on with a high school course for four years, or else they may take a "continuation" course for four years.

For example, if a boy elects to be a carpenter he spends forty hours a week as a carpenter's apprentice. Then for fourteen hours a week he goes to a school where he is taught mechanical drawing, designing, the testing of materials, and any other subjects which bear on carpentering. The time he spends in school is credited on the time sheets of his employer.

So at the end of four years the boy, at eighteen, has been well trained in the practice of carpentering by working at his job, and well schooled in its theory by taking a "continuation" course which bore directly on his work. Thus wage-earning and education are united to produce a well-trained man.

The school problem of the city suburb is very different from that of the mining village, the rural community, the industrial town, or the city. The children have space, good homes, and abundant opportunity to go through high school and even through college. Under these conditions the elementary grades can be directly preparatory for high school work, since six or even seven out of ten children will go to high school.

In the city suburb there need be little specialization in the elementary grades. The high school, with a general course and two or three special courses, can be relied upon for all necessary specific training.

VIII Beginning with Child Needs

In the industrial town, in the city, and in the city suburb the high school is being looked to as the place where specialized training must be given. The trade school can succeed a little, but its effectiveness will always be limited by the narrow technical character of its instruction, which makes the "continuation" school generally preferable. The high school is not a separate institution, but an integral part of the school system. In a high school, therefore, the children should move naturally from the studies of the elementary grades to more advanced studies, but the purpose of both elementary and high schools is the same—the preparation of children for living.

Children have needs which the schools are here to supply. Certain of these needs are common to all children, and to that extent all schools must provide similar training. Other needs, varying with the size and character of the community, call for a like variation in the course of study.

CHAPTER IV

PROGRESSIVE NOTES IN ELEMENTARY EDUCATION

I The Kindergarten

No single chapter can contain all of the progressive notes that are being sounded in American Elementary Education; yet it is possible, after some arbitrary picking and choosing, to describe a number of the most typical and most successful educational innovations. At the bottom of most up-to-date elementary school systems is the kindergarten. Not so often as it might be, but still frequently, the child begins school work there. The games, the songs, the children's sports of these kindergarten years, make a joyous entry-way into the grades. In Gary the kindergarten child sees life. The flowers, leaves, grasses, lichens, fruits, butterflies, moths, and birds are usually brought to the classroom. The Gary children go on expeditions to explore nature's wonderland, besides making excursions to squares, parks, and to the open country. The kindergartners of Cincinnati plant tulip bulbs in the city parks, and visit farms in order to have a chance to meet the farm animals. Singing, visiting, playing, shaping, building, the kindergarten child sees life on many sides. Perhaps, finally, other cities following the lead of Cincinnati will introduce the kindergarten spirit and kindergarten activities into the lower grades where they will clarify an atmosphere, fetid and dank with concepts which to the six-year-old are meaningless abstractions.

II Translating the Three R's

At best the kindergarten reaches but a few. Even in cities which boast of a system of organized kindergartens, only a small portion of the children attend them. On the other hand, since practically all school children enter the grades, it is on them that an inquiry into elementary education must be focused.

The time has passed when reading, writing, and arithmetic made up the entirety of a satisfactory elementary education. Like the kindergarten, the elementary school must touch life; like the kindergarten, it must provide for child needs. Everywhere schools are turning from the old methods of teaching spelling, multiplication, and syntax to the new methods of teaching children,—yes, and teaching them those things which they need, irrespective of name. Three R's no longer suffice. The child requires training from the Alpha to the Omega of life.

Compare, for example, the old method of teaching geography with the new. Under the abandoned system, the child began with capes, peninsulas, continents, meridians, trade routes, rivers, boundaries and products. Under the new system, he begins with the town in which he lives. Each schoolroom in Newark, for example, is provided with a large map of the city. In addition to these complete maps, each child is given a series of small maps, each of which centers about a familiar square, store, or public building. Then, from this simple beginning, the child fills in the surrounding streets and buildings. Newark geography begins in the third grade with a description of the school yard and the surroundings of the school lot. After all, what more simple geography could be conceived than the geography that you already know. Borneo and Beloochistan are abstractions except to the most traveled, but what child has not noted the red bricks and ugly iron fences surrounding his own school yard? Charity and geography both begin logically at home.

When in the later Newark grades the children are taught about Europe and Australasia, they are taught on a background of the geography of yards, alleys, squares, streets and playgrounds with which they are familiar. Geography thus concretely presented, becomes comprehensible to even the dullest mind.

III Playing at Mathematics

The passing system of elementary mathematics took the innocents through addition, subtraction and the abatis of multiplication tables, until every child was fully convinced that

>   Multiplication is vexation,
>   Division's twice as bad,
>   The rule of three perplexes me,

And practice drives one mad.

To-day arithmetic begins with life. The teachers at Gary organize games in which the children are divided into two sides. Some of the children play the game, while others keep score. Unconsciously, under the stress of the most gripping of impulses—the desire to win—these little scorekeepers learn addition. As they advance in the work, they take up practical problems—measure the room for flooring and measure the school pavement for cementing. At school No. 4, in Indianapolis, one of the teachers wanted a cold-frame and a hot-bed for use in connection with her nature work. The class in mathematics made the measurements; the drawing class provided the plans; the boys in the seventh and eighth grades dug the pit and constructed the beds.

The higher grade mathematics work in Indianapolis is extremely concrete. Prices and descriptions of materials are supplied, and the children are asked to compute given problems involving the buying of meats, groceries, and other household articles; the cost of heating and lighting the home; the cost of home furnishing; the construction of buildings; cost-keeping in various factories; the management of the city hospital; the taxation of Indianapolis; the estimation and construction of pavement; and, generally, the mathematical problems involved in the conduct of public and private business.

Mathematics is alive when it is joined to the problem of life. Well taught, it becomes a part of the real experiences of childhood and furnishes a foundation for the knowledge of later life.

IV A Model English Lesson

Of all subjects taught in the schools, English is the most practical, because it is most used in life. We buy with it, sell with it, converse with it, write with it, adore with it, and protest with it. English is the open sesame of life in English-speaking countries. In some classes the English period would be fascinating even for adults.

What experience could be more delightful than a visit to a third or fourth grade room in which the children were writing original poems, fables and stories! The monotony of routine English work was completely broken down; the children were enthusiastic,—enthusiastic to such a degree that they had all written poetry.

Just before Halloween the teacher had distributed pictures of a witch on a broomstick, with a cat at her side, riding toward the moon. Each child was called upon for an original poem on this picture. One boy of eight wrote:—

>   There was an old witch
>   Who flew up in the sky,
>   To visit the moon
>   That was shining so high.

Another child improved somewhat upon the versification—

>   The witch's cat was as black as her hat,
>   As black as her hat was he.
>   He had yellow eyes which looked very wise
>   As he sailed high over the trees.

How many of you mature men and women could have done a better piece of work than Dorothy Hall, nine and a half years old?

THE MOONLIGHT PEOPLE

>   When the stars are twinkling,
>   And the ground with snow is white,
>   And we are just awaking
>   For to see the morning light;
>   Little moonlight people
>   Are dancing here and there
>   O'er a snow white carpet,
>   Dancing everywhere.

This same class of little people, after learning Riley's "Pixie People," were asked to write down what they believed were the circumstances under which Riley composed the poem. Their reasons varied all the way from a dream of butterflies, to cornfields.

Seventh and eighth grade children in this same city (Newton, Mass.) write books, the titles of which are selected by the children with the approval of the teacher. "A Boy's Life in New York," "Fairy Stories," "A Book About Airships," "A Story of Boarding School Life," are a few of the titles. Having chosen his title, the child outlines the work and then begins on it, writing it week by week, illustrating the text with drawings, illuminating and decorating the margins with water colors, painting a tasty cover, and at last, as the product of a year's work in English, taking home a book written, hand printed, hand illumined, covered and bound by the author. Could you recognize in this fascinating task the dreaded English composition and spelling of your childhood days?

One eighth grade lad, who had always made a rather poor showing in school, decided to write his book on birds. As he worked into the subject it gradually got hold of him. In the early spring he found himself, at half past four, morning after morning, out in the squares, the parks and the fields, watching for the birds. He became absorbed in writing his book, but at the same time the teachers of other subjects found him taking additional interest in them. The whole tone of his school work improved; and when, in May, he delivered an illustrated lecture, before one of the teachers' meetings, on the birds of Newton, he was triumphant. In less than a year he had vitalized his whole being with an interest in one study.

"In his talk to the teachers," said Superintendent Spalding, "he showed a deeper knowledge of the subject than most of the teachers present possessed."

Those who remember with a shiver of dread the syntax, parsing, sentence diagramming, paragraph dissecting, machine composition construction of the grammar grades, should have stepped with me into the class of an Indianapolis teacher of seventh grade English. The teacher sat in the back of the room. The class bent forward, attentively listening while a roughly clad, uncouth boy, slipshod in attitude, stumbled through the broken periods of his ungrammatical sentences.

"And Esau went out after a venison," he was saying, "and Jacob's mother cooked up some goat's meat till it smelled like a venison. And then Jacob, he took the venison—I mean the goat's meat to Isaac, and Isaac couldn't tell it wasn't Esau because"—so the story continued for two or three minutes. When it was ended, the boy stood looking gloomily at the class.

"Well, class?" queried Miss Howes, "has any one any criticism to make?"

Instantly, three-quarters of the class was on its feet.

"Well, Edward."

Edward, a manly fellow, spoke quietly to the boy who had told the story.

"Paul, you don't talk quite loud enough. Then you should raise and lower your voice more."

Several of the class (having intended to make the same criticism) sat down with Edward. The teacher turned.

"Yes, Mary."

"Paul, your grammar wasn't very good. You didn't make periods."

One by one, in a spirit of kindly helpfulness, criticisms were made. When the children had finished, Miss Howes said:

"Paul, you did very well. This is your first time in this class, isn't it?"

"Yes'm."

"Yes, Paul, you did very well; but, Paul"—and with care and precision she outlined his mistakes, suggesting in each case ways of avoiding them in the future.

Throughout the grades in Indianapolis the children have some oral English work every day. When they reach the seventh and eighth years this oral work takes on quite pretentious forms. Beginning with Aesop's Fables, the children tell fairy tales, Bible stories, Greek legends, Norse legends, animal stories, and any other stories that the teacher thinks appropriate. Each child may select in the particular group of stories whatever topic seems most interesting.

Each day has its written English work, too. On Monday, letters are written and criticized; Tuesday is composition day; on Wednesday each scholar writes a description of the day in a Season Journal; Thursday is set aside for the revision and correction of compositions; and on Friday, the letters for the following Monday are written. Wherever possible, the subjects for written work are selected with reference to the other studies which the child is taking.

V An Original Fairy Story

The work is arranged primarily to arouse interest. At Halloween, the theme is timely, and one girl, Dorothy Morrison, selects as her title, "How the Witch got the Black Cat for her Prisoner." Read this charming fairy tale—an original piece of work by a girl of twelve:

> "Years ago, when the witch rode her broomstick, no snarling black cat accompanied her on her midnight rides. That wicked person was always planning and plotting how to get some nice young girl to go with her.
>
> "At this time there lived a beautiful fairy, who was condemned to death by a cruel magician, who had no reason to do so. This good fairy, Eilene, finally decided to take the shape of a bird and to fly through the tiny window of her prison to her old friend, Mr. Moon.
>
> "She did so, and when she arrived at her friend's home she assumed the form of a fairy and entreated him to keep her safe from the cruel clutches of the magician.
>
> "He promised to do his best.
>
> "The next Halloween, the witch, Crono, rode up to the moon and on spying Eilene she exclaimed, 'Aha, just what I have been looking for—a nice young maiden.'
>
> "Eilene became frightened at first and clutched the moon's hand. Just then Crono grabbed at her, but she was too quick for her, for she changed herself into a bird and flew out of the reaches of the witch.

"Shaking her fist at the girl she muttered, 'I will get you yet.'

"Then the witch returned to her caldron and Eilene returned to the moon. Mr. Moon then advised her to be careful for Crono wanted her for her prisoner. She did not heed this because she thought that she could outwit Crono with all her fairy power, but she was mistaken, for Crono had more power than she. One day, while sitting at the moon's knee, listening to the story of how he got up in the sky, Eilene's hands and feet were tied, and before Mr. Moon could help her, what little power that fat personage possessed was taken from him.

"Crono transformed Eilene into a snarling black cat which now always accompanies her on her Halloween rides when she tells the grinning Jack-o'-Lanterns of how she captured Eilene.

"Because Mr. Moon loved Eilene so well, Crono gave him a picture of the fairy, which he always keeps near him, and even to this day, if we look up at the moon, we can see the picture of Eilene. So let us remember that, although the black cat does appear fierce, she is really good at heart."

VI The Crow and the Scarecrow

When corn was sprouting, "Crows and Scarecrows" was announced as a topic, and one Irish lad, giving rein to his imagination, wrote:—

THE CROW AND THE SCARECROW

"Having a story to write concerning a crow, I decided to go to the zoological gardens and seek an interview with one of the species. Accordingly I went, and after passing numerous cages containing all kinds of animals, I arrived at the bird cages. Here in one cage all by himself I met Mr. Crow. He was a big bird with coal-black feathers that glistened in the sunlight.

"I made a bow, explained my errand and asked for a story. He cocked his head to one side, looked steadily for a few seconds and then actually winked at me. 'Well, young man,' he said in a throaty voice, 'you have certainly come to the right place. But as it is near my lunch time I must be brief.

"'In the first place, I was the leader of as wild and mischievous a band of crows as you ever heard tell of. There was one particular farm in our territory we loved to visit. The owner's name was Silas Whimple and he was the grouchiest, most miserly man in the county. He lived alone and what part of the ground that was tilled, he did it himself. As much to tease as to eat, we would pay him an occasional flying visit, digging up his newly planted seeds, nibbling at the young green shoots, or, later on, scratching up his potatoes. All his shouting and screaming did not scare us a bit. One day one of my companions came winging with the news that Silas had a farm hand. I laughed and said, "If there is another man on the farm then Silas Whimple must be dead." Off we flew to investigate. Sure enough, out in a patch of potatoes was a man. Watching him quite a while, I saw he did not move or make a noise as Silas would. He just stood still. I came down to take a closer look, when who should come to the doorway but Silas himself. He was laughing and shouting, "Now I have something to keep you away. The scarecrow shall keep you from bothering me any more." He laughed and laughed, but I watched my chance and flew behind this being and scratched off his cap. Then the story was out. It was only a straw man. I went back to my companions and explained, and before evening we had picked the scarecrow to pieces. Next day I was unfortunate enough to put my foot in a wire trap and then they sent me up here for life.'

> "At this moment his keeper came up with something to eat, so I bade him good-bye and left."

English, in these classes, is so alive with interest that the children write with ardor and read eagerly the literature which, improperly handled, they learn so soon to despise.

The time-honored studies of the old curriculum may be charged with interest if they are linked to life. The most irksome task has its pleasant aspects. Even the three R's may be translated into current thought.

VII School and Home

Even more significant for the future is the work which is being done in a few cities to train girls for their chief work in life—homemaking. The home schools at Indianapolis and Providence are, perhaps, typical. The Indianapolis School Board bought a number of wretched homes near one school in a crowded district. The boys in the school renovated the homes, converting one into a rug shop, another into a mop factory, and still a third into a shoe-shop. In these shops the children of the school did their trade work. Another house was made into a model home—(model for that quarter)—in which the domestic science department was located. Of this home the girls took entire charge, living in it by the day. There they were taught, by practical experience, the art of homemaking.

The home school of Providence, Rhode Island, under the direction of Mrs. Ada Wilson Trowbridge, has received nation-wide recognition. Six hundred dollars, appropriated by the Board of Education, renovated and furnished the flat on Willard Avenue in which the school is held.

The girls who elect to take work in the home school—the work is wholly elective—may come on Monday and Tuesday, or on Wednesday and Thursday. The hours are 4 to 6, or 7:30 to 9:30. On Friday, anyone comes who cares to. The day pupils are from the grammar schools and the evening pupils come from the factories and shops. Seventy-five names on the waiting list of day classes indicate the popularity of the school.

"We try to keep the school like the homes from which these girls come," explained Mrs. Trowbridge, as she showed her tastefully arranged apartment. "The girls in the Technical High School worked out the color schemes, selected the patterns and bought the materials. We tried to get things which were good looking and durable."

The three kinds of work, (1) Cooking, (2) Housekeeping, and (3) Sewing, are carried on in rotation, a girl spending one entire afternoon at cooking, the next at sewing and a third at housework. Thus each girl does an afternoon's job in each subject. The cooking class studies successively "breakfast," "lunch" and "dinner," in each case preparing menus and cooking the food. A meal is served nearly every day. The service falls to the housekeeping class, which is also responsible for cleaning up, tending the furnace, washing, ironing and the like. Included in this part of the work are a number of thorough discussions of personal hygiene and home sanitation. To the sewing class, the girls bring their home sewing problems. Certain classes darn stockings while a teacher reads to them. Some girls make underclothing and dresses. The beginners hem table cloths, napkins, towels, dustcloths, etc., for the school. The classes are small (ten to fifteen) making individual work possible.

"No, no," protested Mrs. Trowbridge, "we have no course of study, or else, if you please, there are as many courses as there are girls. Each girl has her problems and we aim to meet them."

The backyard, utilized as a garden, furnishes vegetables which the girls cook and can. These vegetables, together with canned fruits, jellies, jams and pickles, which the girls put up, give the school such an excellent source of revenue that last year it turned over $15 to the Superintendent of Schools.

The crowning work of the school was done in a bare upstairs room which the girls papered and painted themselves. "Two of them have since done the same thing with rooms at home," declared Mrs. Trowbridge, happily. "Isn't that good for a start?"

The home school stays close to home problems, dealing with the facts of life as the girls who come to school see them. It would hardly be fair to expect more of any school.

VIII Breaking New Ground

The regular work of the public school has been supplemented, of late years, by a number of significant innovations, of which the most far-reaching is, perhaps, a medical inspection of schools which involves a thorough physical examination of all school children by experts. By this scheme, the defect of the individual child is corrected, and the danger of widespread contagion or infection in the schoolroom is reduced to a minimum.

Following these physical examinations, the children who are clearly sub-normal are placed in special classes or special schools, where, under the direction of specially fitted teachers, they do any mental work for which they are fitted, in the interims of time between manual activities. Weaving, woodworking, folding and similar employments hold the attention of sub-normal children where intellectual work will not. The special school, freed from the throttling grip of an iron-clad course of study, studies the need of each child, and makes a course of study to fit the need. Although the special school has been used for incorrigibles, its real value rests in its care of the defective child.

Anaemic children and those who show a tubercular tendency are treated in open air schools. In Springfield a special school was constructed. In Providence an old building was employed. In all cases, however, the windows are notable by their absence. The school supplies caps and army blankets, a milk lunch in the middle of the forenoon and the afternoon, and a plain, wholesome dinner at noon. A few months of such treatment works wonders with most of the children. It seems only fair that the sick school child should be treated to fresh air and full nutrition, even though the well child is not so favored.

The open air school has borne fruit, however, in the establishment of numerous open-window classes. Against these classes, there seems to be only one complaint. The children are too lively. Fancy! They get a supply of oxygen sufficient to stimulate them into life during school hours. How tragic this must seem to the teacher who is in the habit of calming the troubled spirits of her class by a generous administration of closed windows and carbon dioxide.

A few cities are attempting to relieve underfeeding by the provision of wholesome school lunches at cost. Buffalo leads in the work, with Chicago, Philadelphia and a number of other cities trailing behind. When you remember that the Chicago School Board reported that in the Chicago schools there were "five thousand children who were habitually hungry," while "ten thousand others do not have sufficient nourishing food," you will perhaps agree that the time has come for some action.

Among the liveliest educational movements of the day is that of providing school children with a legitimate occupation and a convenient place to be occupied outside of school hours. Chicago, with an unequaled system of playgrounds, and Philadelphia, with a department devoted to school gardens, are leaders in two fields which promise great things for the future welfare of American city school children.

IX The School and the Community

Not content with doing those needful things involved in the education of children of school age, the school is reaching far out into the community. Night schools came first, as a means of education for those who could not attend school during the daytime. Every progressive city and town has a night school now, and the scholars who come after working hours use the same expensive equipment that is furnished to the regular classes. Machines, cooking apparatus, maps and blackboard all do double duty. In the foreign quarters, particularly, the night schools attract a large following of adults, eager to learn the language and ways of the new land. Though many a one falls asleep over the tasks, who shall say that the spirit is not willing?

Public lectures are being used more and more as a means of public education. There is scarcely an up-to-date city that has not some public lectures connected with its school or library system, while in a center like New York, the Board of Education has established an elaborate organization for the delivery of lectures in public school buildings throughout the city. The lecture topics—widely advertised through the schools and elsewhere—cover every field of thought.

Perhaps the whole movement of the schools to influence the community may be summed up in the phrase, "A wider use of the school plant." Why should not the schools be open, as they are in Gary, day and evening, too? Why should the mothers and fathers not be organized into "Home and School Leagues," meeting in the schools as they do on a large scale in Philadelphia? Why should not the social sentiment of a community be crystallized around its schoolhouse, as it has been in Rochester? Is it better to have the children playing in the street in the summer time, or in the school yards and playgrounds, as they do in Minneapolis and St. Paul?

The billion dollars invested in the school plant must be made to yield a return in broader social service with each succeeding year.

X New Keys for Old Locks

Nor have progressive educators been satisfied to change the methods of teaching old subjects. More important still, they have introduced new courses which aim to open larger fields for child experience. Hygiene, nature study, civics, manual training and domestic science have all been called upon to enrich the elementary school curriculum.

The nineteenth century physiology—names of muscles and bones, symptoms of diseases and the like—has been replaced in the twentieth century schools by a physiology which aims to teach that the body is worth caring for and developing into something of which every boy and girl may be proud. Beginning with nature study and elementary science, the hygiene course in Indianapolis emphasizes, first, the care of the body and then, in the seventh and eighth grades, public health, private and public sanitation, etc. From nature and her doings, the child is led to see the application of the laws of physiology and hygiene to the life of the individual and of the community.

Nature study, elementary science, horticulture and school gardens have taken their place, on a small scale, in all progressive educational systems. There is an education in watching things grow; an education in the sequence and significance of the seasons, which brick and cement pavements can never afford.

Scattered attempts are being made to teach children the relation between individual and community life. All of the seventh and eighth grade children in Indianapolis visit the city bureaus—water, light, health, fire and police. Trips to factories teach them the relation between industry and the individual life, while social concepts are developed by newspaper and magazine reading, book reading and class discussions of the articles and books which are read. At election time they discuss politics; they take up strikes and labor troubles; woman suffrage is occasionally touched upon; and they are even asked to suggest methods of making a given wage cover family needs.

The widespread introduction of domestic science and elementary manual training renders any special discussion of them unnecessary. In some instances, however, they are developed to a high degree. In Gary, Indianapolis and Cincinnati, seventh and eighth grade girls make their own garments, cook and serve meals to teachers or to other classes; while in the advanced grades the boys make furniture, sleds, derricks, bridges and telegraph instruments. Chair caning, weaving and clay modeling are also widely used in the hand work of both boys and girls.

Fitchburg, Mass., has developed a Practical Arts School, paralleling the seventh and eighth grades in the grammar school. The school includes a Commercial Course, a Practical Arts Course, a Household Arts Course and a Literary Course. The regular literature, composition, spelling, mathematics, geography, history and science of the seventh and eighth grades is supplemented by social dancing, physical training and music in all of these courses; and in addition for the Commercial Course by typewriting, shorthand, bookkeeping, business arithmetic and designing; for the Practical Arts Course, by drawing, designing, printing, making and repairing; for the Household Arts Course, by cooking, sewing, homekeeping and household arts; and for the Literary Course, by half-time in modern language and the other half in manual training and household arts.

At the end of the sixth year (at about twelve years of age) children in Fitchburg may elect to take this school of Practical Arts instead of the regular grammar school course. The results of this election are extraordinary. The practical course was planned for the children who expected to leave school at fourteen, or at the end of the eighth grade. Curiously enough, all types of children have flocked into it. Sons of doctors, lawyers and well-to-do business men; boys and girls preparing for college, and children who must stop school in a year or two are all clamoring for admission. In spite of the fact that pupils are kept in these schools six hours a day instead of five, as in the other schools, the attendance at the end of two years has outrun the accommodations. The children who leave this applied work and enter the high school are apparently not a whit less able to do the high school work than those children who have come up through the regular grades.

The new education is broader than the old, because it accepts and adopts any study which seems likely to meet the needs or wants of any class of children or of any individual child. The storehouse of the mind is to-day unlocked with educational keys of which educators in past generations scarcely dreamed.

XI School and Shop

For the present, at least, there are a great number of children who must leave school at fourteen, whether they have completed the grammar grades or not. With them, the problem of education shapes itself into this question: "Shall they be well or badly prepared for their work?" The boys enter the shops and mills; the girls marry and make homes. Are they to be efficient workers and housekeepers? The answer rests largely with the schools.

Ohio has provided, for the solution of the problem, a continuation school law, modeled on the more extensive plans of the German Continuation School system. The law reads: "In case the board of education of any school district establishes part-time day schools for the instruction of youths over fourteen years of age who are engaged in regular employment, such board of education is authorized to require all youths who have not satisfactorily completed the eighth grade of the elementary schools to continue their schooling until they are sixteen years of age; provided, however, that such youths, if they have been granted Age and Schooling Certificates and are regularly employed, shall be required to attend school not to exceed eight hours a week between the hours of 8:00 A. M. to 5:00 P. M. during the school term."

Cleveland and Cincinnati, acting under this authority, have established continuation schools. In Cleveland they are voluntary; in Cincinnati they are compulsory. In both cities, children between fourteen and sixteen may attend school, during factory time, for four hours each week.

Little enough, you protest. Yes, but it is a beginning.

The child in such a continuation school may choose between academic work, art, drawing and designing, shop-work, millinery, dressmaking and domestic science. In some cases a continuation course is possible. Thus far the system has worked admirably.

Equally significant are the Massachusetts Vocational Schools, which are intended to provide a technical training for the boys who wish to pass directly from the grammar school into industry.

Under the Massachusetts law, the state pays half of the running expenses of any vocational school which is organized with the approval of the State Director of Vocational Training. The Springfield school, under the supervision of E. E. MacNary, is housed on one floor of a factory building. The boys may not come at an earlier age than fourteen and Mr. MacNary insists, where possible, that they complete the regular seventh grade work before coming to him. His school, which includes pattern making, cabinet work, carpentry and machine shop work, is run on the "job" plan. That is, a boy is assigned to a job such as making a head-stock for a lathe. The boy makes his drawings, writes his specifications, orders his material and tools, estimates the cost of the job, makes the head-stock and then figures up his actual costs and compares them with the estimated cost. Not until he has gone through all of the operations, may he turn to a new piece of work.

"We tried the half-day and half-day in shop plan," Mr. MacNary explains, "but it was not a success. It disturbed the boys too much. So we hit on the plan of letting each boy divide his time as he needed to. When he has drawing and estimating to do, he does that and when the time for lathe work comes, he turns to that. It breaks up any system in your school, but it gives the best chance to the individual boy."

One day a week all of the boys meet the teachers in conference to discuss their work and to make and receive general suggestions.

The boys who come to Mr. MacNary's school are boys who would probably leave the regular school at fourteen. Many boys come because they are discouraged with the grade work, and of these "grade failures," many succeed admirably in the new school. During the two years of this shop-work, the boys get a training which enables them to take and hold good positions in the trades. As one foreman said, "A boy gets more training in the two years of that school than he gets in three years of any shop."

These are but an index of the myriad of attempts which cities are making to bring school and shop together, to train for usefulness, to start boys in life.

XII Half a Chance to Study

There are other ways in which the school may help. For example, in the case of homework. On the one hand, homework for the sake of homework may be eliminated. On the other hand, children may be given half a chance to read and study.

One day in a squalid back street I glanced through the window of a corner house. The front of the house was a grocery store. The room into which I happened to look was a general dwelling room. On one side stood the kitchen stove; the floor was littered with children and rubbish, and just under the window a child sat, her book before her on the supper-covered dining table, doing multiplication examples—her homework. The well-to-do child, less than ten squares away, who bent over her problems in a quiet room, could scarcely appreciate the difficulties attached to homework, when the family lives in three rooms and does everything possible to reduce the bill for kerosene.

There is just one place in every neighborhood where the child can find light, air and quiet—that place is the school. Why then should the school not be open for the child? "Why, indeed," asked the schoolmen of Newark, N. J. Passing from thought to deed, they opened schools in the crowded neighborhoods four nights a week from 7 to 9.

Into these evening study classes, in charge of advisory teachers, any child might come at all. The city librarian, generous in co-operation, lent library books in batches of forty, for two months at a time. Evening after evening, the boys and girls assemble and with text-books or library books, do those things in the school which are impossible in the home. For what other purpose should the school exist?

XIII Thwarting Satan in the Summer Time

Another project, equally effective, involves the opening of schools during the summer time. The farmer needed his boy for the harvest, so summer vacations became the established rule, but the city street needs neither the boy nor the girl at any time of the year. Idleness and mischief link hands with street children and dance away toward delinquency. Then why not have school in the summer time? Why not?

The answer takes the form of vacation schools. In most cases the work of the vacation school is designed primarily to interest the child. Games, stories, gardening, manual work of various sorts, excursions and similar devices are relied upon to maintain interest.

A few cities, like Indianapolis, Worcester and Gary, on the other hand, have established vacation schools in which children may make up back work, or pursue studies in which they are especially interested.

As a means of bringing below-grade children up to the standard of affording an opportunity for the able children to advance more rapidly in school, and, in general, as a means of keeping city children usefully occupied during the summer months, the vacation school has won its place.

Newark, making an even more radical departure from tradition, runs some schools twelve months in the year. Edgar G. Pitkin, principal of a school in an immigrant district, first put the idea into practice. At the end of the regular session in June, he announced to his children that school would start again on the following Monday. Fearfully he approached the building. The streets about the school seemed unusually deserted that Monday morning. Suppose no one should be there! When the gong sounded, however, more than seven-tenths of the two thousand children belonging in the school were in their places. The attendance that summer was ninety-two per cent, and the promotion ninety-five per cent. During the three summer months there were exactly two cases of discipline.

"You see what happened," Mr. Pitkin explained. "All of the bright ambitious children came back and the loafers stayed away. From that picked crowd nothing but good work could be expected. There was no attendance officer on duty, but the children were regular. Order was so good that on hot days we put up the sashes between rooms, and on the second floor, where four class-rooms were thrown into one, four classes worked industriously under four teachers without the least friction."

This school has been organized on a year schedule. If the children come four terms each year instead of three, they will reduce the time between the first and eighth grades by one-third, which means a saving to them and to the school. Since it is the able children who come, the twelve months' school affords them an opportunity to go quickly through work on which the slower classmates must hold a more moderate pace.

XIV Sending the Whole Child to School

It is a long step from the school of—

> Reading, and writing and 'rithmetic,
> Taught to the tune of the hickory stick,

to the school which aims at the education of the whole child; yet that step has been attempted in Gary, Indiana. There, perhaps more consistently than anywhere else in the United States, the school authorities are providing for the whole child in their schools. Many schools have manual training and domestic science; many schools have school gardens and playgrounds; many schools have nature work in the parks and squares; but in no school that I have visited did I find a more conscious effort to unite mental and physical, hand and head, and vocation and recreation, in one complete system.

This result, which to some may sound unbelievably like the impossible, is accomplished first, by engaging experts to teach such special subjects as botany and physical training; second, by abolishing grade promotions and permitting each child to advance in his subject when he is ready to do so; third, by keeping the school open morning, afternoon and evening during practically the entire year; fourth, by making the work of interest to each individual child. Perhaps this matter of interest sums up better than any other the spirit of the Gary schools. The system aims to make the school so attractive that children will prefer to be there rather than to be anywhere else.

How is this done? Take the case of John Frena, who occupies a place of no particular distinction in the fifth year of the Gary schools. John's school day (from 8:30 A. M. to 4:00 P. M.) is divided equally between regular work (reading, writing, geography, etc.) and special work (play, nature study, manual training and the like). A day of John's school life reads like this:

> *First period*—Playground, games, sports and gymnastics, under the direction of an expert.
>
> *Second period*—Nature study, elementary science and physical geography.
>
> *Third and fourth periods*—Reading, writing, spelling and language.

Lunch hour.

Fifth period—Playground (as before).

Sixth period—Drawing and manual training.

Seventh and eighth periods—History, political geography and arithmetic.

During his school day, John has played, used his head and his hands, and alternated the work in such a way that no one part of it ever became irksome.

Next week, music and literature will be substituted on John's program for drawing; the following week manual training will replace one period of play. The four special subjects (drawing and manual training, music and literature, nature study and science, and plays and games) rotate regularly. Each day, however, includes four periods of this special work and four periods of regular work.

Such a plan sounds complicated. In reality, it is very easy. The gymnasium teacher stays in the gymnasium, the drawing teacher in the drawing room. In the regular work, there are forty children in each class. For science and manual training these classes split in two. At the end of each period, or of each two periods, depending on the subject, the children pass from one room to another. While this system brings them under several teachers each day, it enables them to take a subject like art with one teacher for twelve years.

Meanwhile our little friend John has shown himself bright in language, but slow in arithmetic. Immediately he is advanced in language, and perhaps placed in a lower arithmetic class. He may even be transferred to another teacher for special arithmetic work. The system permits this flexibility because it allows each teacher, an expert in her own field, to shape her work to suit her pupils.

Better still, if John cannot master his arithmetic in the regular classes, he may attend voluntary classes on Saturday, at night, or during the summer months. The schools afford him every chance to keep up in every subject, and if he cannot make his way in this subject or in that, he works in the fields which are open to him, doing what he can to make his course a success.

John, in the schools of Gary, is John Frena, with all of John Frena's limitations and possibilities. The Gary school seeks to bridge the limitations, expand the possibilities, and give John Frena a thousand and one reasons for believing that if there is any place in the world where he can grow into a complete man, that place is the Gary school.

XV Smashing the School Machine

One of the oft-repeated complaints against the old education arose from the iron-clad system of promotion which once in each year, with automatic precision, separated the sheep from the goats, saying to the sheep, "go higher," and to the goats, "repeat the grade."

For the sheep, the system worked fairly well, at least that once; but for the goats, it was a tragedy. The child who had failed in one out of six branches, side by side with the child failing in six out of six, repeated the year.

The new education affords several remedies for this situation. Of these the most generally known is promotion twice yearly. While this affords considerable relief, it is greatly improved upon in Springfield, Mass., by the division of each grade into three divisions—advanced, normal and backward. These divisions the teacher handles separately so that when promotion time comes the children who have shown special aptitude are prepared to go into the next grade. Meantime the children have been constantly changing from one division in the class to another.

Perhaps the most generally practicable plan for relieving the mechanical features of promotion is found in Indianapolis, and even more intensely in Gary, where children are promoted by subjects rather than by grades. In Indianapolis, the child entering the sixth grade, takes all English with one teacher from that time until the end of the eighth grade. If the child is strong in English, he advances rapidly. If he is weak in English, the teacher gives him special attention. Learning each pupil's capabilities in her particular branch, the teacher is able to give the individual child, over a series of years, the help which his special case requires.

In Gary the departmental idea is carried through the entire school system. In the Emerson School, for instance, children may take eighth grade work in English and high school work in nature study or history. The departmental work is strengthened in Gary, in Indianapolis, and in a number of other cities, by afternoon work, Saturday classes and vacation schools. Here, a child interested in any phase of the school work or desiring to make up work in which he is deficient, may spend his spare time to his heart's content.

An even greater individuation of children exists in Fitchburg and Newton, Mass., and in Providence, R. I. Children from the country and foreign children who have difficulty with their English, together with any other children who do not fit into any grade, are placed in an ungraded class. A typical ungraded class of fifty pupils contained Germans, Russians, Greeks, French, Italians and Polish children, who were unable to speak English on entering the school. The ages of these children varied from eight to fifteen. As soon as the ungraded children appear to be fitted for any special grade, they are transferred.

This ungraded work is supplemented by "floating teachers," who are located in each school for the purpose of dealing with special cases. The case of any child who, for this reason or that, cannot keep up with the work in a particular subject, is handed over to these teachers. Thus individual attention is secured in individual cases.

XVI All Hands Around for An Elementary School

These progressive educational steps are not isolated instances of success in new lines, nor are they incompatible with good work. They may be welded into a unified system, aglow with the real interests of real life. It is possible to correlate the old standard courses and the new fields in such a way that the child will gain in interest and in life experience.

Nowhere is this possibility better illustrated than in the elementary schools of Indianapolis. Take as an example School No. 52, which is located in an average district. The children, neither very rich nor very poor, possess the advantages and disadvantages of that great mass known as "common people."

The children in grades one to three, inclusive, in addition to studying the three R's, spend thirty minutes each day learning to measure, fold, cut and weave paper. In grades four and five, an hour and a half per week is devoted to simple weaving, knife-work, raffia work, sewing and basketry. Grade six has four and a half hours of similar work each week, while in grades seven and eight, the pupils are occupied for one-third of their entire school time in art work, book-binding, pottery work, weaving (blankets and rugs), chair caning, cooking, sewing and printing.

"But how is it possible?" queries the defender of the old system. "How can the necessary subjects be taught in two-thirds of the time now devoted to them? Are we not already crowded to death?"

Yes, crowded with dead work, the proof of which lies in the fact that the children who devote a third of the time to apply their knowledge get as good or better marks in the academic work than the three-thirds children. That, however, is not the really important point. This course of study is valuable because it gives a rounded, unified training.

This is how the course is organized. The school life is a unit, into which each department fits and in which it works. The spelling lesson is covered in the classroom and set in type in the print shop. The grammar lesson consists in revising compositions with regulation proofreaders' corrections. The art department designs clothes which are made in the sewing classes. The drawing room furnishes plans for the wood and iron work and designs for basketry and pottery. In the English classes, the problems of caning and weaving are written and discussed. The mathematical problems are problems of the school. Children in the sixth year keep careful accounts of personal receipts and expenditures—accounts which are balanced semi-weekly. The boy in one woodworking class makes out an order for materials. A boy in another class makes the necessary computations and fills the order. All costs of dressmaking and cooking materials are carefully kept and dealt with as arithmetic problems. For the older boys, shop-cards are kept, showing the amount and price of materials used and the time devoted to a given operation. These again form a basis for mathematical work. The whole is knit together in a civics class, which deals with the industrial, political and social questions, in their relations to the child and to the community.

Best of all, the things which the children talk and figure about, plan and make, have value. The seventh and eighth year girls make clothes which they are proud to show and wear; they cook lunch for which some of the teachers pay a cost price. The baskets are taken home. Eighty chairs are caned by the children each year. The bindery binds magazines, songs and special literature. The boys make sleds and carts, hall stands, umbrella racks, center tables and stools. They make cupboards and shelves for the school, quilting-frames on which the girls do patchwork. Rags are woven into rag carpets and sold. The print shop prints all of the stationery for the school. Each can of preserves, in the ample stock put up by the girls, is labeled thus:

"Preserved Peaches"

with labels printed by the boys.

June, 1912, witnessed a triumph for the entire school. The children in the upper class had taken up the study of book-making. They even went to a bindery and saw a book bound and lettered. Then, to show what they had learned, they composed, set up and printed—

A Book
About Books
by
June 8 A Class

This book of twenty-eight pages, tastefully covered and decorated, contained three half-tone cuts which the children paid for by means of entertainments; an essay by Hazel Almas on "The History of Books," one by Adele Wise on "The Printing of a Book," and one by Ruth Kingelman on "The Art of Bookbinding"; the program of the commencement exercises, and a collection of poems and wise sayings.

The children went further and invited Mr. Charles Bookwalter, the owner of the bookbindery where they had learned their lesson, to come and talk to them on Commencement Day. He came, made a splendid address and went away filled with wonder before these achievements of fourteen-year-old grammar school children.

Each grade has a special subject of study. This year the boys in the Eighth A are studying saws; the boys in Eighth B, lumbering; the girls in Eighth A are investigating wool and silk; while in Eighth B the girls are studying cotton and flax. This "study" means much. Not only do the children discuss the topics, write about them, read books on them, and do problems concerning them, but they visit the factories and study the processes from beginning to end.

When the problem of pins came up, the teacher desired several copies of a description of pin-making, so she asked the class to write out a letter to the manufacturers. The class, left to select, decided to send this letter:

SCHOOL No. 52,

Indianapolis, Ind.,

Oct. 11, 1912.

AMERICAN PIN COMPANY,
    Waterbury, Conn.

Dear Sirs: On seeing the pamphlet on pins you have been kind enough to send us, I have decided to write and ask you if you would kindly send us about twenty of your pamphlets on the making of pins.

We are in the eighth grade, and expect to go out into the world in January, and your process of making pins will be spread abroad to the whole world.

We are very anxious to know more about the making of pins, and we are very much interested in your process.

Yours sincerely,
RUTH HARRISON.

Need I say that the American Pin Company sent immediately twenty duplicates of the desired pamphlet?

The work in this school where thought and activity go hand in hand, is done by the regular grade teachers—done, and done well. They are as enthusiastic as the pupils. Four years' trial has convinced them. On the day that I visited the school, I walked into a classroom where twenty girls were busy sewing. The order was perfect. Every one was busy. The teacher was nowhere in evidence.

"That teacher," explained the principal to me later, "is off at a teachers' meeting. She left these girls on their honor to work. You see the result."

I saw and marveled. Yet why marvel? Was not this a typical product of the system which knits thought and activity into such a harmonious, fascinating whole as the most fortunate adults find in later life? Out of such a school may we not well develop harmony and keen life? Never yet have men gathered grapes from thistles, but often and often have they plucked from fig trees the figs which they craved and sought.

XVII From a Blazed Trail to a Paved Highway

Pages might be filled with descriptions of similar successes, yet I think that my point is already sufficiently established. How can we disagree regarding so plain a matter? The path of educational progress has led away from the three R's along a trail, blazed at first by a few men and women who dreamed and stepped forward hesitatingly. Often they retraced their steps, discouraged, and gave over the little they had gained. By degrees, however, the trail was blazed. The way became clearer. After all it was possible to connect education with life.

Slowly the light of this truth dawned upon men's minds. Gradually the way opened before them. One by one they trod the path, bridging the worst defiles, straightening the road, cutting out the thickets and filling in the morasses, until at last, behold the way, explored by hesitating, derided pioneers, no longer a trail, but a broad highway. Others have gone—their name is legion—and have succeeded. The three R's are but the beginning of an adequate elementary curriculum. You, in your own city, with your own teachers, can vitalize your elementary schools. You can teach the children to use their heads and hands together, and thus show them the way to a deeper interest in your schools, and a larger outlook on their work in life.

CHAPTER V

KEEPING THE HIGH SCHOOL IN STEP WITH LIFE

I The Responsibility of the High School

"Every pupil of high school maturity should be in high school atmosphere whether he has completed the work of the grammar grades or not," insists Dr. F. E. Spaulding. "Perhaps the high school course of study is not adapted to the needs of such children. Well, so much the worse for the course of study. The sooner the high school suits its work to the needs of fourteen and fifteen-year-old boys and girls, the sooner it will be filling its true place in the community." Such opinions, voiced in this case by a man whose national reputation is founded on his splendid work as superintendent of the school system of Newton Mass., bespeak the attitude of the most progressive American high schools.

The high school is not a training ground for colleges, nor is it a repository of classical lore. As an advanced school it differs no more from the elementary school than the six cylinder automobile differs from the four cylinder car. Though its work is more complex, like the elementary school it exists for the sole purpose of helping children to live wholesome, efficient lives.

II An Experiment in Futures

Children who get stranded in the seventh or eighth grades may have failed in one subject or in several. Over age and out of place, they lose interest, become discouraged and at fourteen drop out of school to work or to idle. In Newton, as in every other town, there were a number of just such children whom Mr. Spaulding decided to get into the high school.

"There they will be among children of their own age," he explained. "They may take a new line of work and acquire a real interest."

"But they will fail in their high school work as they have failed in their grade work," protested the doubters.

Mr. Spaulding, smiling his quiet, genial smile, tried his experiment all the same. From the seventh and eighth grades of the Newton schools he picked the boys and girls who were fifteen or more at their next birthdays. These pupils, seventy in all—forty girls and thirty boys—were transferred, without examination, into the high school.

"These youngsters were going to drop out of school for good in one year, or two at the outside," explained Mr. Spaulding, "so I made up my mind that during that year at least they should have some high school training. They went to the regular high school teachers for their hand-work; but for their studies, I put them in charge of three capable grade teachers, who were responsible for seeing that each child was making good. I put it to the grade teachers this way: 'Here are a lot of children who have got the failure habit by failing all through their school course. Unless we want to send them out of our school to make similar failures in life, we must teach them to succeed. Take each child on his own merits, give him work that he can do and let him learn success.'

"We gave these boys and girls twenty hours a week of technical work (drawing, designing, shop-work, cooking and sewing) and ten hours a week of academic work (English, mathematics, civics and hygiene). Shop costs, buying of materials and simple accounting covered their mathematics. Those were the things which would probably be most needful in life. The boys got deeply interested in civics, and we let them go as far and as fast as they pleased. With the girls we discussed hygiene, dressing and a lot of other things in which they were interested.

"When those children entered the school they were boisterous and rough. The girls dressed gaudily, reveling in cheap finery. By Christmas, to all appearances, their classes differed in no way from the other high school classes. They all brushed their hair. The boys were neater and the girls were becomingly dressed.["]

Most of the seventy children stayed through the year. Twenty-seven of the forty girls and seventeen of the thirty boys entered the regular high school course the next fall. They were thus put into competition with their former seventh and eighth grade comrades, although they had had only two-fifths as much academic work as the regular eighth grade pupils. There was the test.

Could these derelicts, after one year of special care, take their places in the regular freshman high school work? After the end of the first quarter, a study made of the 800 children in the high school showed that on the average there were fifty-four hundredths of one failure for each scholar. Among the twenty-seven girls from the special classes, however, there was but seventeen-hundredths of a failure for each girl, or one-third as many failures as in the whole school. The boys made an even better showing. Of the entire seventeen, only one boy failed, and in only one subject.

III The Success Habit

"We had given them something they liked and could do," Mr. Spaulding concluded. "They succeeded a few times, got the success habit, learned to like school, went into the regular high school course and succeeded there."

As an illustration of the way in which the new plan works, take the case of James Rawley. James was in a serious predicament. Time after time the court had overlooked his truancy and misdoings, but James had taken the pitcher once too often to the well, and the open doors of the State Reform School stared him grimly in the face.

"It will be best for him in the long run," commented the judge. "Each month of this wild life makes him a little less fit to keep his place in the community. He has had his last chance."

Yet there was one ray of hope, for James lived in and out of Boston, a city located near the Newton Technical High School. This fact led James's custodians to propose to the judge that he give James one more trial, this time in the Newton Technical High School. The judge, also of the initiated, agreed to the suggestion, and James, a dismal eighth grade failure, entered the Newton Technical High School in one of the special transfer classes.

Just a word about James. He began life badly. His mother died when he was young; and his father, a rather indifferent man, boarded the boy out during his early years with an aunt, who first spoiled him through indulgence, and then, inconsistently enough, hated him because he was spoiled. Growing up in this uncongenial atmosphere, James became entirely uncontrollable. He was disagreeable in the extreme, wild and unmanageable.

The people with whom James was boarding grew tired of his continued truancy and he was placed on a farm near Boston. There, too, he was discontented, dissatisfied and disobedient. Time after time he ran away to Boston. He went on from bad to worse, falling in with vagrants, learning their talk and their ways, acquiring a love for wandering and a distaste for regularity and direction. Taken into custody by the Juvenile Court, and placed on probation with a family outside of Boston, James again ran away to mingle with a crowd of his old associates in Boston. It was at this point that the court decided to send him to the Reform School. It was likewise at this time that some friendly people took him in charge, found him a home in Newton, and started his life anew in the Newton Technical High School, which James entered with a special transfer class. Promoted to the regular freshman class on trial, James has renewed his interest in education and bids fair to make his way through the high school.

James is doing well in the Newton Technical High School. Though he does not like all of the regular high school work, he has a full course, and is working at it persistently. Heretofore school has never appealed to him—in fact, he hated it cordially—but the school at Newton offered him such a variety of subjects that he was able to find some which were attractive. Since then he has been working on those subjects.

There are many cities in which every school door would have been closed to James, because he did not fit into the school system, but the superintendent of the Newton schools believes in making the school fit the needs of the boy. A fantastic theory? Well, perhaps a trifle, from one viewpoint; nevertheless, it is the soul of education.

IV The Help-Out Spirit

As a result of this special promotion policy, there are practically no over-age pupils in the grammar schools of Newton. Instead of square pegs in round holes, the Newton High School can boast of sixty or seventy children who come, each year, in search of a new opening for which they are technically not ready, but into which they may grow. After coming to the high school, two-thirds of them find an incentive sufficient to lead them to continue with an education of which they had already wearied.

The Newton High School, recognizing its obligation to serve the people, strains every nerve to enable boys and girls to take high school work. The printing teacher pointed to his class of twenty.

"Only three of them do not work on Saturdays and after school. They couldn't come here if they didn't work. Hiney, there, was in a bakeshop all day at three and a half a week. We got him a job afternoons and Saturdays that pays him three dollars. That tall fellow will send himself through high school on the six dollars a week that he gets from a drug store where he works outside of school hours."

"We aim," added Mr. Spaulding, "to do everything in our power to make it possible for the boys to come here. If their parents cannot afford to send them, we find work for them to do outside of school hours."

That is virile work, is it not? And the result? During the past eight years the number of pupils in the Newton schools who are over fourteen has increased three times as fast as the number of pupils who are under fourteen. The school authorities have searched the highways and byways of the educational world until one-quarter of the school children of Newton are in the high schools.

V Joining Hands with the Elementary Schools

The same result which is attained informally at Newton is accomplished more formally by the organization of the junior high schools which have sprung up in Berkeley and Los Angeles, California; Evansville, Indiana; Dayton, Ohio, and a number of other progressive educational centers. The child's school life under this plan is divided into three parts—the elementary grades (years one to six), the junior high school (years seven to nine) and the high school proper (years ten to twelve). The break, if break there must be, between the elementary and the high school, thus comes at age twelve and at age fifteen, instead of, as formerly, coming at age fourteen, when the temptation to leave school is so strong. Then, too, the sharp transition from work by grades to work by departments is made easier because the junior high school combines the two, leading the pupil gradually over from the grade method to the department method.

Though the junior high school has so great a popularity, its work is eclipsed by the still more revolutionary program of those educators who advocate the complete abolition of any line between the elementary and the high school, and the establishment of a public school of twelve school years. This plan, coupled with promotion by subjects rather than by grades, replaces the machine method of promotion and the gap between elementary and high schools by an easy, natural progression adaptable to the needs of any student, from the end of the kindergarten to the beginning of the university.

Superintendent Wirt of Gary, Indiana, has established such a twelve-year course in the Emerson School. The grades, numbered from one to twelve, are so arranged that a girl may take half of her subjects in school year eight (last grammar grade) and the other half in school year nine (first high school grade). In order to make the harmony more complete, Mr. Wirt places the elementary rooms, containing the second grade pupils, next door to the rooms which shelter high school seniors. On this side of the hall is a kindergarten; directly across from it is a class in high school geometry.

The same plan, on a larger scale, has been adopted by I. B. Gilbert, principal of the Union High School, Grand Rapids, Michigan, which houses twelve hundred students.

"We have obliterated the sharp line of distinction between the grades," declared Mr. Gilbert. "The school, which is a new one, has a very complete equipment—physical, chemical, and biological laboratories, two cooking rooms, dressmaking and millinery rooms, an art department, a woodworking shop, a forge room and a machine shop; the print shop, though not yet installed, is to be put in this year. By bringing children of all grades to the school, we place at the disposal of grade pupils apparatus ordinarily reserved for high school pupils only. At the same time, our equipment is in constant use and the cost of establishing a separate industrial department or school for the grades is eliminated.

"These are merely the surface advantages, however. The real gain to the students is in other and most significant directions. First, the abolishing of rigid grading allows each child to follow his own bent. At the beginning of the adolescent period, when the old interests begin to lag, some new ideas must be furnished if the child is to be kept in school. We provide that new stimulus by beginning departmental work with the seventh year (at twelve or thirteen). Then, if the child shows any particular preference for any line of work, he may pursue it. From the seventh grade up, promotion is by subjects entirely, and not by grades. If a student elects art, she may follow up her art work for the next six years; similarly, a boy may follow shop-work, or a girl domestic science or millinery. In order to fit the school more quickly to the pupils' need, we make a division at the beginning of the eighth grade of those pupils desiring to take academic work and those desiring to take industrial work in the high school. The latter group does extra sewing or shop-work twice each week.

"Again, we take all over-age and over-size pupils from the schools in this section of the city, and by placing them in ungraded classes, permit them to take the work which they can do. Here is a boy who cannot master grammar. That is no reason why he should not design jewelry, so we give him fourth year language, and take him into the tenth year class in jewelry design. Yes, and he makes good, doing excellent craft work and gradually pulling up in his language. By this means we make our twelve grade school fit the needs of any and every pupil who may come to it.

"We have a natural educational progress for twelve years," concluded Mr. Gilbert. "There is no break anywhere. Instead of making it hard to step from grade eight to grade nine, we interrelate them so intimately that the student scarcely feels the change from one to the other. The result? Last June there were 152 pupils in our eighth grade. Of that number 118, or more than three-quarters of them reported in the ninth grade this fall. We have cancelled the invitation to quit school at the end of the eighth grade and our children stay with us."

VI The Abolition of "Mass Play"

Thus the dark narrow passage-way from the elementary to the higher schools is being widened, lighted, paved and sign-posted. In some school systems it has disappeared altogether, leaving the promotion from the eighth year to the first year high school as easy as the step from the seventh to the eighth grade. After the children have reached the high school, however, the task is only begun. First they must be individualized, second socialized, and third taught.

"The trouble with the girls," complained Wm. McAndrew, in discussing his four thousand Washington Irvingites, "is that they have always been taught mass play. Take singing, for instance. A class started off will sing beautifully all together, but get one girl on her feet and she is afraid to utter a note. The grade instruction has taught them group acting and group thinking. I step into a class of Freshmen with a 'Good morning, girls'.

"'Good morning,' they chorus.

"'Are you glad to see me, girls?'

"'Yes sir,' again in chorus.

"'Do you wished I was hanged?'

"'Yes sir,' generally,—

"'Oh, no sir,' cries one girl who has begun to cerebrate. The idea catches all over the class, and again the chorus comes,—

"'Oh, no sir, no sir.'

"So it goes. The bright girl takes her cue from the teacher and the class takes the cue from the bright girl. They must be taught to think and do for themselves."

Everyone interested in school children should visit the Washington Irving School (New York) and watch the truly wonderful McAndrew system of individualization. In the office, you are cordially greeted. You wish to see the school? By all means! But no teacher is detailed to serve you. Instead, a messenger goes in search of the Reception Committee. Two of the school girls, after a formal introduction, start your tour of inspection, if you are fortunate enough to be there at nine, with a visit to one of the assembly rooms, where, in groups of three or four hundred, the girls enjoy three-quarters of an hour each morning. The word "enjoy" is used advisedly, for, unlike the ordinary assembly, this one is conducted entirely by the girls.

Each morning a different chairman and secretary is selected, so that in the course of the year every girl has had her turn. The chairman, after calling the meeting to order and appointing two critics for the day, reads her own scripture selection, and then calls upon some girl to lead the salute to the flag. The minutes of the previous day's meeting are then read, discussed and accepted. After fifteen minutes of singing—singing of everything from "Faust" to "Rags"—the chairman calls on the two critics for their criticism of the conduct of that day's meeting. Some special event is then in order. On one Monday in December Miss Sage, head of the Biology Department, described the Biological Laboratory in the new school building. After she had finished, the chairman rose.

"Will anyone volunteer to tell in a few words the principal points which Miss Sage made?"

Three girls were promptly on their feet, giving, in clear, collected language, an analysis of the talk.

After you, as a guest, have been conducted to the platform, introduced to the chairman, and given a seat of honor, the chairman turns to the assembly, with the announcement,—

"Girls, I wish to introduce to you our guest of this morning."

Instantly the whole assembly rises, singing blithely, "Good morning, honored guest, we the girls of the Washington Irving High School are glad to welcome you."

The proceedings having come to an end, the chairman declares the meeting adjourned and you look about, realizing with a start that the girls—freshmen, sophomores, juniors, and seniors—have spent three-quarters of an hour in charge of themselves, and have done it with interest, and with striking efficiency. Continuing your journey, you find the process of individualization everywhere present. Here a girl is in front of a class, directing the calisthenics which precede each class hour. There a girl is standing at the front of the room, leading singing or quizzing in geometry.

"Yes, it was a wrench," Mr. McAndrew admits. "You see, the teachers hated to give up. They had been despots during all of their teaching lives, and the idea of handing the discipline and a lot of the responsibility of the school over to the girls hurt them dreadfully, but they have tried it and found that it works."

VII Experimental Democracy

The high school pupil, after discovering himself, must next determine his relation to the community. It is one thing to break down what Mr. McAndrew calls the W. I. (Wooden Indian) attitude. It is quite another to relate pupils to the community in which they live. Yet this, too, can be done. The school is a society—incomplete in certain respects, yet in its broad outline similar to the city and the state. The social work of the school consists in showing the citizens of the school-community how to enjoy the privileges and act up to the responsibilities of citizenship. The Emerson School at Gary and the Union High School at Grand Rapids, organized into complete schools from the first grade to the end of the high school, are miniature working models of the composite world in which all of the children will live.

Particularly effective work has been done on the social side of high school organization at the William Penn High School (Philadelphia), where Mr. Lewis has turned the conduct of student affairs over to a Student Government Association, directed by a Board of Governors of eighteen, on which the faculty, represented by five members, holds an advisory position only. The Association gives some annual event, like a May day fete, in which all of the girls take part. It assumes charge of the corridors, elevators, and lunch rooms; grants charters to clubs and student societies, and assumes a general direction of student affairs.

"It really doesn't take much time," Irene Litchman, the first term (1912-13) President, explained. "We like it and we're proud to do it. We used to have teachers everywhere taking charge of things. Now we do it all ourselves." True enough, Madame President, and it is well done, as any casual observer may see. Similar testimony is to be had from the sick girls who have received letters and flowers, from the children whose Christmas has been brightened by Association-dressed dolls, and from the girls whose misunderstandings with members of the faculty have been settled by the Student Association.

Each class in the Washington Irving High School (New York) gives one reception a term to one of the other classes. In addition, an annual reception and play are given by the entire school. The plays for these occasions are written, costumed and staged by the students. Last year the reception was given to Mrs. Dix, wife of the Governor of New York, and the play "Rip Van Winkle" was acted by eighteen hundred girls. Such organizations and activities lead high school students to feel social relationships, and to assume responsibilities as members of the social group.

VIII Breaching the Chinese Wall of High School Classicism

A high school education is included, by progressive communities, in the birthright of every child. Since only a small part of these children are preparing for college, the school must offer more than the traditional high school course. The principal of a great Western high school which housed nearly two thousand children, pointed to one room in which a tiny class bent over their books. "That is probably the last class in Greek that we shall ever have in the school," he said. "They are sophomores. Only two freshmen elected Greek this fall, and we decided not to form the class." Time was when Greek was one of the pillars of the high school course of study. In this particular school, splendidly equipped laboratories, sewing rooms, and shops have claimed the children. The classics are still popular with a small minority, but the vast majority come to learn some lesson which will direct their steps along the pathway of life.

Everywhere the technical high school courses are gaining by leaps and bounds. The William Penn High School (Philadelphia), established in 1909, is to-day enrolling four-fifths of the girls who enter Philadelphia high schools. In some cities, technical work and classical work are done in the same building; in other cities, they are sheltered separately, but everywhere the high school is opening its doors to that great group of school children who, at seventeen or eighteen, must and will enter the arena of life.

The technical high school has not gained its prestige easily, however. The bitter contests between the old and the new are well portrayed by one dramatic episode from the history of the Los Angeles High School. Mr. John H. Francis, now superintendent of the schools of Los Angeles, was head of the Commercial Department in the Los Angeles High School. Despite opposition and ridicule the department grew until it finally emerged as a full-fledged technical high school, claiming a building of its own,—a building which Mr. Francis insisted should contain accommodations for two thousand students. The authorities protested,—"Two thousand technical students? Why, Los Angeles is not a metropolis." Mr. Francis gained his point, however, and the building was erected to accommodate two thousand children. When the time for opening arrived it was discovered, to the astonishment of the doubters, that more students wanted to come into the school than the school would hold. When Mr. Francis announced that students up to two thousand would be admitted in order of application, excitement in school circles ran high, and on the day before Registration Day a line began to form which grew in length as the day wore on, until by nightfall it extended for squares from the school. All that night the boys and girls camped in their places, waiting for the morning which would bring an opportunity to attend the technical high school.

Though less dramatic in form, the rush toward technical high school courses is equally significant. It is not that the old high school has lost, but that the new high school is drawing in thousands of boys and girls who, from lack of interest in classical education, would have gone directly from the grammar school into the mill or the office.

IX An Up-to-Date High School

The modern high school is housed in a building which contains, in addition to the regular class rooms, gymnasiums, a swimming tank, physics, and chemical laboratories; cooking, sewing, and millinery rooms; wood-working, forge, and machine shops; drawing rooms; a music room; a room devoted to arts and crafts; and an assembly room. This arrangement of rooms presupposes Mr. Gilbert's plan of making the high school, like the community, an aggregation of every sort of people, doing every sort of work.

Physical training in the high school has not yet come into its own, though it is on the road to recognition. All of the newer high schools have gymnasiums, but the children do not use them for more than thirty, forty, or fifty minutes a week. Sometimes the work is optional. The West Technical of Cleveland, with its outdoor basket ball court, its athletic grounds and grandstand, in addition to the indoor gymnasium, offers a good example of effective preparation for physical training. William D. Lewis of the William Penn High School sends all students who have physical defects to the gymnasium three, four, or even five times a week, until the defects are corrected. These exceptions merely serve to emphasize the fact that we have not yet learned that high school children have bodies which are as much in need of development and training as the minds which the bodies support.

Several real attempts are being made to teach high school boys and girls to care for their bodies, as they would for any other precious thing. Hygiene is taught, positively,—the old time "don'ts" being replaced by a series of "do's." In many schools, careful efforts are being made to give a sound sex education. The program at William Penn, in addition to the earlier work in biology and in personal and community hygiene, includes a senior course, extending through the year, in Domestic Sanitation and Eugenics. The course, given by the women in charge of Physical Training, deals frankly with the domestic and personal problems which the girls must face. The time is ripe for other schools to fall in line behind these much-needed pioneers.

The course of study in the modern high school is a broad one. Latin may always be taken, and sometimes there is Greek. French, German and Spanish, Mathematics, History, Physics, Chemistry, Biology, and Civics are almost universally offered on the cultural side of the curriculum. In addition, girls may take dress designing, sewing, millinery and home economics; boys may take wood-working, forge work, machine-tool work, electricity, printing, and house designing; and both boys and girls have an opportunity to elect art, arts and crafts work and music.

In some schools the combination of subjects group themselves into definite courses, as in the Newton High School, which offers,—

> The Classical Course.
> The Scientific Course.
> The General Course.
> The Technical Course.
> The Technology-College Course.
> The Extra Technical Course.
> The Fine Arts Course.
> The Business Course.

Other schools, like the Indianapolis Manual Training School, permit the pupil, with the advice of the principal, to make his own combination of subjects. Whether prepared by the school or by the pupil, however, the courses lead to college, to normal schools, to advanced technical schools, or to some definite vocation. On one subject, progressive high schools are in absolute agreement,—the course of study must furnish both culture and technical training in a form which meets the needs of high school children.

X From School to Shop and Back Again

The tendency toward vocational training finds its extreme expression in the so-called Industrial Co-operative Course in which boys and girls spend part of their time in school and part in the factory. Note this legal document. "The party of the second part agrees to place, as far as possible, the facilities of his establishment at the disposal of the School Committee for general educational purposes along industrial lines." In these words, the individual manufacturers of Providence, Rhode Island, who are co-operating with the school board for the establishment of the industrial co-operative course in the Technical High School, place their mills and factories at the disposal of the school authorities. The plan instituted at the suggestion of the manufacturers themselves has won the approval of all parties during the two years of its operation.

The Providence experiment differs from those of Cincinnati and Fitchburg, Mass., in two respects,—in the first place, the school authorities have a written contract with the manufacturers. In the second place, they may decide what the character of the shop-work shall be. The boy who elects to take the industrial co-operative course in Providence spends ten weeks in a shop at the end of his freshman year. Apprenticeship papers are signed, the boy gives a bond, which is forfeited if he drops the course without a satisfactory reason, and for three years he spends 29 weeks in the shop and 20 weeks in school, alternating, one week in the shop, the next in the school. For their shop-work the boys receive ten cents, twelve cents, and fourteen cents an hour during the first, second, and third years, respectively. Though this wage is not high, it is sufficient to enable the boys to earn enough during the year ($175 to $250) to pay for their keep at home during their high school course.

At the present time sixty-two Providence boys are working part time in machine shops, in drafting rooms, in machine tool construction, in pattern making and in jewelry making. In order to keep the scheme elastic, the school offers to form a class in any trade for which sixteen or more boys will apply.

The part-time course is primarily educational and secondarily vocational. Since it may determine the character of the shop-work, the school is in a position to insure its educational value. Again, the academic training is still received in the school, while the technical work, heretofore done in school rooms, is carried on in the fields of real industry. As a supplement of the old time system of apprenticeship, the part-time school is an undoubted success, because it adds to shop apprentice work all of the essential elements of a high school education.

XI Fitting the High School Graduate Into Life

The high school has not done its full duty when it has educated the child,— it must go a step farther and educate him for something; then it must go a step beyond that and help him to find himself in his chosen profession. This vocational guidance which is filling so large a place in public discussions, may mean guidance to a job or it may include guidance in the job. In either case children must be led to decide upon the kind of work for which they are fitted before they leave the school.

Jesse B. Davis, Principal of the Central High School at Grand Rapids, furnishes a brilliant example of this vocational directing. Mr. Davis begins his work through the theme writing and oral composition of the seventh and eighth grades. The purpose of the pupils' reading and discussion is to arouse their vocational ambition and to lead them to appreciate the value of further education and training for life. This study upon the part of the pupil is supplemented by talks given by Mr. Davis, prominent business and professional men and high school boys who have come back to finish their education after a few years of battle with the world.

The high school classes in English are small—never more than twenty-five, and the work is so arranged that the teacher may get a good idea of the capability of each student. To facilitate this, the English Department has prepared a series of essay subjects in the writing of which the pupil gives the teacher a very definite idea of himself. Beginning with "My Three Wishes;" the pupil next writes a story about his ancestry; an essay on "My Church," which explains his belief; an essay on "The Part I'd Like to Play in High School;" a study of "My Best Friend," and finally an essay on "The Work of My Early School Days," which shows the pupil's likes and dislikes. In addition to this, the teacher notes any physical defects—eyesight, hearing, and the like—which might incapacitate the pupil for particular vocations. This data, together with reports from all departments on neatness, sincerity, ambition and other qualities is filed in the office.

During the second term of the freshman year papers are written on approved biographies, dealing in each case with the qualities, opportunities and education of the great one. These essays, read in class, form the basis for a compilation of the elements necessary for success in life.

The work of the sophomore year begins with the preparation of a class list of professions, semi-professions and trades,—a list which is checked with the permanent list kept by the department. Succeeding classes thus discover the breadth of the vocational field, besides adding to the knowledge accumulated by their predecessors.

After completing this list, the pupils write a letter to the teacher, choosing a vocation and assigning reasons for the choice. When the pupil cannot decide, the teacher assigns the vocation apparently best suited to the pupil's capacity. An essay on his vocation is then prepared by each pupil, showing first, what kind of activity and what responsibilities the vocation involves; second, its social, intellectual and financial advantages; third, the corresponding disadvantages; fourth, the qualifications and traits necessary to success in the vocation; and fifth, the reasons for choosing the vocation. Then, under the advice of the teacher, the pupil writes to some man well known in the profession of his choice—some lawyer, mining engineer, doctor or contractor—explaining what he is doing, and asking for advice. The generous responses given by men in all walks of life do much to confirm the pupil in his faith, or to make him see that his choice is an unwise one.

At the beginning of the junior year those pupils preparing for college send for the catalogues of the colleges which stand highest in the line of work in which they are interested, and write an essay, giving the comparative value of the courses offered by the various institutions. By this means judgment takes the place of sentiment in the selection of a college. While the college preparatory pupils are engaged in writing on their college courses, pupils who are going directly from the high school into business write an elaborate essay on the kind of preparation necessary for their vocation, the qualities requisite for success in it, and the best place and means of entering it. Studies of the proper relations between employer and employed occupy the second half of the junior year.

The work of the senior year deals, in the first half, with the relation between a citizen and his city; the second half, with the relation between a citizen and the state. The pupil has thus passed from the narrower to the broader aspects of his work in life.

The effectiveness of the work is enhanced by the organization of the high school boys into a Junior Association of Commerce (in an exact imitation of the Grand Rapids Association of Commerce), which meets in the rooms of the latter on Saturday morning; transacts business; listens to an address by a specialist, and then visits his works, if he is engaged in a local industry. On the Saturday before Thanksgiving (1912), for example, Mr. VanWallen, of the VanWallen Tannery Co., gave the boys a talk on the tanning industry, then took them through his tannery, where they saw the processes of manufacture. The business men of Grand Rapids, who are highly pleased with this practical turn in education, co-operate heartily in every way. The boys are urged, during the summer months, to take a position in the work which they have chosen, start at the bottom and find out whether their beliefs regarding the industry are true. Then, too, the Free Library makes a point of collecting books and articles on various professions and vocations, and placing them prominently before the students. The English Department (with five periods a week) does other work, but none so vital to the pupils' lives as this of directing them in the thing which they hope to do when they leave school.

The school may do more than direct the pupils in the choice of their occupations, by actually securing positions for them. The head of the Commercial Department in the Newton (Massachusetts) High School has a card for every student, giving on one side a record of class work for four years, and on the other side a statement of positions and pay of the graduate. New pupils are placed; old pupils are offered better opportunities. Employers are interviewed in attempts to have them promote graduates. Through this system, Mr. Maxim keeps in constant touch with the labor market and with graduates of his school.

Certainly the high school must prepare students for life. Whether, in addition, it shall constitute itself a Public Employment Bureau, finding positions for students, keeping in touch with their careers, and assisting in their advancement, is a matter yet to be determined.

XII The High School as a Public Servant

Will the high school retain its present form? Probably not. If the Berkeley-Los Angeles plan prevails, there will be three steps in the public schools,—from elementary to junior high, to high school. If the Gary plan wins, there will be twelve years of schooling, following one another as consecutively as day follows night. Whether the Los Angeles or the Gary plan is adopted, one thing seems reasonably certain,—the high school will keep in close touch with life.

The high school is securing a surer grip on the world with each passing day. It is reaching out toward the grades, calling the pupils to come; it is reaching out into the world, making places there for them to occupy. The modern high school has ceased to be an adjunct to the college. Instead, it is a distinctive unit in educational life, taking boys and girls between the ages of fourteen and nineteen and relating them to the world in which they must live.

The era of the high school course is being succeeded by the era of the high school boy and the high school girl. First, last, now and always, the boys and girls, not the course, deserve primary consideration. Whatever their needs, the high school must supply them if it is to become a public servant, responsible for training children of high school age in the noble art of living.

CHAPTER VI

HIGHER EDUCATION AT LOWVILLE[20]

I Lowville and the Neighborhood

Away off in northwestern New York State, where the sun shines fiercely in the summer mid-day, where the ice forms thick on the lakes, and the snow lies on the north side of the hills from Thanksgiving well on to Easter, there is a town of some three thousand inhabitants, called Lowville. The comfortable homes, brick stores, wide tree-bordered streets, smiling hills and giddy children look very much the same at Lowville as they do in any one of a thousand similar towns east of the Mississippi. Situated far back from the line of ordinary travel, the town is typical of a great class.

Stretching in all directions about Lowville is a fertile, prosperous, agricultural region, farmed by good farmers, who are intelligently awake to the problem of scientific agriculture in its multiple phases.

These farmers grow fruits, raise general farm produce, breed a little stock, cut some timber, besides all of the time-honored occupations of the professional farmer. The boys and girls growing up in the town or the neighboring countryside, blessed with good air, and a cheap supply of wholesome food, look pleasantly forward toward life as something worth living.

So much for the good side of Lowville. Sad indeed is it to recall that there is another side. Anyone who has been in close contact with country life can readily imagine the ignorance, bigotry, prejudice, unfairness and unsociableness of the population; the tendency to cling to the past no matter what its shortcomings; the unwillingness to venture into even the rosiest future which involves change. Lowville is blessed a great deal and cursed a very little. The blessings are being augmented and the curses minimized by means of the local high school.

II Lowville Academy

Lowville Academy is an ancient private school whose usefulness was immensely enhanced when it was converted into a public high school. When Mr. W. F. H. Breeze took over the principalship he made no particular objection to the old class rooms and wooden stairs, but he was very insistent upon discovering, first, what the community needed, and second, whether or not the school was meeting the need.

More than half (at the present time sixty-five per cent.) of the pupils at the school came from outside of the village. That is, they come from the farms. As farmers' boys, many of them have been brought up to all of the unscientific crudities which have been handed down in American agriculture since the early settlers took the land from the Indians in grateful recognition of their instructions in fertilization. While many agricultural anachronisms may be laid to the door of the redskins, planting by the moon and several equally absurd customs are traceable to the higher civilization of Western Europe.

Saturated with traditional agricultural lore—some better and some worse—the boys and girls from outside of Lowville, sixty-five in each hundred high school students, were growing up to become the owners of promising New York farms. They needed, first of all, an education which should equip them with all of the culture of our schools, beside giving them a knowledge of the sciences of agriculture and of mechanics. Those boys and girls who were planning to go to college required an advance course in those purgatorial topics which, for some inexplicable reason, are still regarded as necessary preliminaries to a college education. Most of the girls in Lowville and the immediate vicinity hope to marry sooner or later, and to preside over wholesome, clean homes. For home-making, also, there were certain possible educational provisions.

As prospective farmers, mechanics, college students, business men and women, as prospective fathers and mothers, the boys and girls of Lowville were looking to the schools—high as well as elementary—for an education which should enable them to do successfully and efficiently those things which life was holding before them.

Furthermore, Lowville had no spot around which community interests and civic ideas could center. There was intelligent interest in Lowville, its streets, schools, trees, houses, and business interests; there was, too, an interest, expressed among the neighboring farmers, in the wonderful strides of agriculture; furthermore, men and women were anxious to discuss political and social happenings in other parts of the world.

What more natural than that the school be converted into a center of interest and education for Lowville and the surrounding territory. Adults, as well as young folks, needed school help. Adults as well as young folks should then be accommodated in the Lowville schools.

III The School's Opportunity

"There was a peculiar opportunity," said Mr. Breeze, in his crisp direct way. "The place needed organizing in educational lines. People were anxious to have it done. They wanted the advantage of a modern educational institution, but no one had provided it, so I made up my mind that my business was to do it."

Mr. Breeze made his first innovation in the course of study, supplementing the old course by domestic science, several phases of agriculture and mechanics. Then he correlated the various branches in such a way that the subjects all harmonized with the work which any particular student was doing.

"We made up our minds," Mr. Breeze explained, "that if we were to hold the children and to educate them usefully, we must make our course fit the things which they had to do in life. The work must come down to earth. It had to be practical—that is, applicable to everyday affairs. Some people confuse practical with pecuniary. There is no relation between the two words. Practical means usable. We set out to make a usable education."

"No education is usable which has frills," Mr. Breeze insists. "Frills are nice for looks, but you can't put on frills until you have a garment to which they may be attached. Our school is providing the garment—we will leave the frills to some one else."

With this idea in mind, the applied courses in the school were organized. Wood-alcohol cook stoves, such as those used in the village, ordinary sewing machines, typewriters for the commercial course, and the simplest tools for the machine shop, made up the equipment.

"These boys have but a few tools at home," Mr. Breeze says. "When they go on the farm they will be compelled to use these tools. Why, then, should they be taught mechanics with tools which they cannot duplicate on their farms without an unjustifiable extravagance?"

IV Field Work as Education

Pursuant to such philosophy, the boys began their shop-work by equipping the shop, building benches, tool-chests, cabinets, and saw horses; putting lath and plaster on the ceiling; setting up the simple tools and putting the shop in running order. Meanwhile, the agricultural students set up two cream separators and a milk-tester, and arranged their laboratory. Then the school was ready for applied work, or rather, the students having graduated from a course in shop equipment, were ready for shop practice.

The entire class in agriculture makes inspection of nearby farms—here to see a well-managed orchard, there a new type of cow-barn or silo. Again they inspect the soil of a district, going carefully over it, picking samples and testing them on return to the school. In fruit-packing season, the students visit the packing houses, or else, in the case of some of the boys, they take a week of employment with a good fruit packer. In season they practice tree pruning, grafting, budding, transplanting and spraying. Whenever possible, the applied work of the school is done in connection with the real applied work of life.

The physics and chemistry are both related to the agriculture and the mechanics courses in the most intimate manner. From the earliest lessons in physics through analyses of heat, light and the principles of mechanics, the theories are constantly interpreted in practical problems which arise in the daily work of the Lowville farmer. The physics teacher, enthusiastic over his students and his work, builds machines and testing devices, which the boys and girls use in solving the problems which they bring from their homes. No less close to the life of the place is the chemical laboratory, which offers opportunity for the analysis of soil, the chemistry of fertilizers, experiments in testing food and milk, and a number of other matters pertaining to agriculture and domestic life.

The mechanical courses are closely related to the work in agriculture, since most of the boys who take up the mechanical work are to go on the farms. The course in mechanics passes quickly over the elements of the work—most boys have learned to use saw, plane, chisel, auger, and hammer years before. The smithing work of tempering, annealing, welding, soldering and removing rust, all leads up to the real work of the shops,—the making of products. The boys make pruning knives, squares and drawing boards, grafting hooks, nail boxes, apple-boxing devices (for this is an apple country), cement rollers, mallets, whiffle-trees, bob-sleds, holders for saw filing, bag-holders, chicken-coops, poultry exhibit boxes, hammer handles, greenhouse flats. Besides, they have exercises in belt-lacing, in cement work, and reinforced concrete. Then, too, they make models of barns and bridges, computing strains, lumber-costs, labor-costs, floor spacing and arrangement.

The agricultural course deals, in some detail, with fruit-growing, animal husbandry, grain-growing, and related topics. Though the scope of such a course is necessarily limited in a high school, it forms an invaluable addition to the knowledge of the boy who cannot go to an agricultural college before he begins his life on the farm. Taught by an agricultural expert, the work assumes real importance to the prospective farmer.

Nor are the girls of Lowville neglected.

V Real Domestic Science

The domestic science department, in charge of an expert, takes up household economics, sewing, dietetics and cooking. The work throughout is practical, the girls learning the principles of sanitation, and their application to the household; domestic art and home decoration; lighting, heating and ventilation. The sewing classes cover the usual exercises in simple hemming and darning, making towels, hemming napkins, and the like; then underclothes, and later dresses are made.

In the cooking laboratory the girls learn food values and food combinations, the cooking of simple dishes, the preparation of entire meals. The girl who finishes the domestic science course in the Lowville Academy is competent to organize a home, cook, sew, keep house and make as efficient use of her opportunities as does her brother who has been trained in mechanics or agriculture.

It is not in the applied courses alone that an extraordinary amount of co-operation has been attained. The academic branches, likewise, are so adjusted as to bear directly upon the work of the remaining courses. The Academic co-ordination is particularly noticeable in the English work, which is required of everyone during the entire high school course. English composition is made to serve as a connecting, co-ordinating study—related to all of the other courses in the school.

The student in agriculture writes reports on various phases of agricultural work, collecting them in a folder and arranging them in order, according to subject. Chemistry reports, history reports, all are made a legitimate part of the work in English.

The results of this system have been more than satisfactory to Mr. Breeze and his staff of co-workers. Students who would have left at the end of the grammar school, are attracted by the high school program, and "saved" by a high school course. The appeal of the school is a wide one. There are no class of boys and girls in Lowville who cannot find something worth while in the high school. Often a student otherwise not brilliant will succeed remarkably in a particular line. Of one such boy in particular Mr. Breeze spoke.

VI One Instance of Success

"He had no taste for Greek, but his reports and analysis in agriculture and mechanics were brilliant. The excellent drawing and sketching and the careful work showed how much appeal the applied course had made to his mind; yet but for the agricultural course he would never have come to high school. A farmer's son with little taste for the ordinary academic studies was inspired by the idea of improved, scientific farming and was getting a thorough insight into the principles of agriculture, chemistry, physics, and mechanics, which will be of the greatest service to him when he takes up farming. Such topics as judging the age of cows, breed of cattle, cost of milk production, the cost of cow-barn construction, grain, hay, cattle rations, silage, and nutrition will all bear directly on the work of the farm in which he is so deeply interested."

So much for the contribution of the Lowville High School to the students who have gone out of its class-rooms and class excursions, stronger in body and more alert of mind. No less remarkable has been its service to the community. At the suggestion of the school authorities acting in co-operation with the Grange, the State, and several other agencies, Lowville has secured an agricultural specialist, whose business it is to travel through the countryside, advising farmers, discussing their problems and suggesting better methods of operating the farms, or of experimenting in new directions. Each winter for one week, a school for adults is held, with courses in agriculture for the men and courses in domestic science for the women. The teachers,—experts from the Cornell School of Agriculture,—are exceptionally well prepared to deal with the problems of New York State farmers.

Higher education at Lowville is education for everyone in Lowville and vicinity who wants it. With one eye on community needs and the other on the best means of supplying them, the Lowville Academy is giving to the citizens of Lowville a twentieth century higher education.

FOOTNOTES:

[20] Much of the material in this chapter appeared originally in the Journal of Education.

CHAPTER VII

A GREAT CITY SCHOOL SYSTEM[21]

I "Co-operation" and "Progressivism"

If any two words in the English language can express the spirit of the Cincinnati schools, they are "co-operation" and "progressivism." The people of Cincinnati, high and low, have banded themselves together in an endeavor to make good schools. Cincinnati schools are not a monument to any individual or group of individuals, rather they are the handiwork of the citizenship. In their eagerness for educational progress, the people are not hypnotized by every cry of "lo here! lo there!" nor do they live in terror of new educational ideas. Their one aim, the education of Cincinnati's children, takes precedence over every other consideration. Perhaps that fact explains both the co-operation and the progressivism.

Co-operation in the educational work of Cincinnati has been developed to a remarkable degree. "There is not a civic society in the whole town which is not working with the schools," says former Superintendent Dyer. Mr. Dyer might have left out the word "civic" and still have been very close to the truth.

Mr. Frederick A. Geier, a leader among the manufacturers who have made possible the "half time in shop, half time in school" system, says of his activity in co-operating with the school authorities: "As a citizen of Cincinnati, I am interested in the schools for two reasons: first, because good schools will bring under their influence the maximum number of pupils and parents, and it is the best agency I can conceive of for producing a high quality of citizenship; second, as a manufacturer I feel that the material prosperity of a community is directly related to the mental and manual equipment of its people." Showing his faith by his works, Mr. Geier has labored in season and out of season to make the schools of Cincinnati the most progressive in the country.

Speaking as "a woman and mother," Mrs. Isabella C. Pendleton, of the Civic League, which has played an active part in building up school sentiment, says: "I consider that the most important features of our school system are the manual training for boys and the domestic science for girls. I am happy to say that to-day a girl on graduating from our schools is capable of taking care of a home." As public schools go, that is not an insignificant achievement. No wonder Mrs. Pendleton, a woman and mother, is interested in schools which accomplish such vital results.

From what extraordinary sources do the schools in Cincinnati secure their support! "All of the local dentists have been brought into close contact with the school system by the efforts of the Dental Society to introduce mouth hygiene into the schools," says Dr. Sidney G. Rauh. "We dentists," adds Dr. Rauh, "are firm believers in general co-operation." No less cordial is the Board of Health in its endorsement of the schools, and in its efforts to raise the health standard of school children.

"I do not believe there is any city in the United States which offers as good an example of the spirit of co-operation as Cincinnati does," affirms Carl Dehoney, of the Chamber of Commerce. "Why are we so active in co-operating with the schools? Simply because we realize that good schools, and especially practical schools, which will fit young men and women for their real life work, have a tremendous bearing upon the efficiency of the people of the city." Mr. W. C. Cauldius, also of the Chamber of Commerce, says: "Our school development is the result of a few years of public support and sympathy." In similar enthusiastic words the leaders of every phase of Cincinnati life express their interest in educational progress.

II An Educational Creed

Let no one infer from what has been said that the people of Cincinnati are agreed upon all of the details of educational policy, nor upon the fundamentals either, for that matter, but they have adopted an educational creed which runs about as follows:

1. I believe in making the schools provide for the educational necessities of every child.

2. I believe that this can be done when all work together.

3. I believe that new ideas are the life-blood of educational advance.

That simple creed adopted by teachers, principals, mothers, manufacturers, dentists and trade unionists has become a great motive force in the upbuilding of the Cincinnati schools.

The most evident thing about the Cincinnati school organization is its democracy. The feudal spirit of lordship and serfdom existing in many schools between superintendents and principals on the one hand, and teachers on the other, is nowhere evident in the Cincinnati schools; instead, each teacher, thrown upon her own initiative, is a creative artist, solving her particular problem as she believes that it should be solved, and abiding by the consequence of her failure or success.

Early in his work Mr. Dyer made it clear that he would not tolerate a mechanical system of education. "Up here on the hill, in a wealthy suburban district, is a grammar school. Its organization, administration and course of study must necessarily differ from that other school, located in the heart of the factory district. The principal of each of these schools has a problem to face—each will succeed in proportion as he grasps the significance of his own problem and the readiest means for its solution." Is not that a refreshing sentiment from a superintendent of city schools? Note this other delightful touch: "My teachers soon learned that I regard the teacher who works exactly like another teacher as pretty poor stuff." Before the axe of such incisive radicalism, how the antiquated structure of the old school machinery came crashing to the ground, to be replaced by a system which recognized each teacher as an individual builder of manhood and womanhood, working to meet the needs of individual children. It is not an idle boast which the English make when they glory in the absence of a curriculum; for even the best curriculum, if mismanaged, is speedily converted into a noose, the knot of which adjusts itself mechanically under the left ear of teacher and child alike. The school authorities of Cincinnati destroyed both knot and rope by giving to their teachers and principals this injunction: "Make your school fit the needs of your children and your community."

The old-time, machine-minded school superintendent, filled with the spirit of co-operative coercion, assembles his teachers. "Now let's all work together," he exclaims, "Here, Susie Smith, this is what you are to teach your pupils, and this is the way in which you are to do it." It was in quite a different spirit that Mr. Dyer said to each one of his teachers: "You do your work, I'll do mine, and together we will make the schools go." It was in this spirit that the teachers were called together to confer on the reorganization of the course of study. Each teacher in each grade had her say in the matter. If the most insignificant teacher in Cincinnati said to Mr. Dyer: "I have an idea that I think would improve the work in my grade," his invariable reply was: "Then try it. There is no way to determine the value of ideas except to try them." By that policy Mr. Dyer surrounded himself with a group of vitally interested people, each one suited to the task in which he believed implicitly, and each one fully convinced that the success or failure of that part of the Cincinnati school system with which he was immediately concerned, depended directly upon his efforts. No wonder the schools succeeded!

III Vitalizing the Kindergarten

The kindergartens are at the basis of the educational system of Cincinnati, and they are in charge of a woman who believes in herself and in her work. Perhaps the people of Cincinnati are not justified in believing that their kindergartens are the very best in the whole United States, but Miss Julia Bothwell, who directs them, says, modestly enough, that she has visited kindergartens in many cities, adopting their schemes and improving in response to their suggestions, until she is convinced that no other city in the land can show a better kindergarten system than that of Cincinnati. In truth, her plan is ordinarily referred to as the "Cincinnati idea."

Cincinnati children begin their kindergarten work at four and a half or five, entering the first grade at six. While in the kindergarten they play the games and sing the songs that all kindergartens play and sing, but with this difference: their plays and songs are built around the things that they do.

The yellow October leaves of Cincinnati's parks half shadow the activity of the busy classes of little kindergarten folks who go there to work and to learn. The Park Commissioners, like every one else in Cincinnati, are in thorough sympathy with the work of the schools, so they allot to each kindergarten class a plot in the park, in which the children—using all of the tools themselves—plant tulip bulbs under the direction of the park gardeners.

"Tulips are the first thing up in the spring," Miss Both well explained, "so we have decided to use them. For years we tried gardens, but children of kindergarten age are not willing to give gardens as much attention as they require; then, too, the gardens ran wild during the summer, so we have settled on the tulip. After the children have planted the bulbs they sing and talk about their work. Then, early in the spring, they begin to visit their plots, watching the first shoots of green as they appear, looking eagerly for the buds, and then, at last, as the reward of their interest, picking the flowers and taking them home. Thus, each child, during his kindergarten course, sees the complete cycle from bulb to flower."

Besides this flower-culture in the park, the children grow hyacinths in the school rooms, visit the woods to collect autumn leaves and spring flowers, make excursions to the country, where they may see animals and crops, and always, for a few days after an excursion, talk about the things which they saw, draw them, sing about them and play games about them. In order to facilitate the work the Board of Education leases a farm, to which the kindergartens go in succession. By these means the life of the city kindergarten child is thoroughly linked with nature.

These things are not new in kindergartening, however. They have merely taken firm root in the fertile soil of Cincinnati's educational enthusiasm. The real excellence of Miss Bothwell's experiment consists in connecting the kindergarten with the early elementary grades on the one hand and with the community on the other.

The first grade children of Cincinnati come back to the kindergarten teachers for an hour's kindergartening once each week, in order to clinch the kindergarten influence on the lives of the first graders. The first grade teachers meet the director of kindergartening once each week, for a discussion of kindergarten methods, and an initiation into the kindergarten spirit. Thus the lump of first grade abstraction is leavened with the leaven of kindergarten concretes, and the grade teachers get the spirit of kindergarten work. In the near future Miss Bothwell hopes to have the kindergarten work extend to the second grade, in order that the spirit, rhythm, harmony and joy of the kindergarten may thoroughly permeate the roots of the Cincinnati school system.

Even more significant—if anything could be more significant than the breakdown of the ironclad, first grade traditions—is the grip which the kindergartens of Cincinnati have secured on the people. The Cincinnati kindergartener is more than a teacher—she serves many masters. In the morning she holds kindergarten classes. On two afternoons a week she does kindergarten work with first grade children; on one afternoon she holds a conference with the supervisor; on a fourth afternoon she visits the classes of first grade teachers or confers with mothers' clubs, and on her remaining afternoon she visits her children in their homes. Out of these varied duties has come: first, a group spirit among the kindergarteners, built upon frequent interchange of plans and ideas; second, an understanding of the relation between the problems of the kindergarten and the problems of the grades; third, a sympathetic grasp of the home conditions surrounding the life of many a difficult child; and fourth, sixty-one mothers' clubs, one organized in connection with each kindergarten, which furnish a social gathering-place for mothers, an opportunity to influence parental ideas, and a body of invaluable public sentiment.

The idea of a kindergarten, usually regarded as a small part of the school program, has been evolved until, in this one city, it is a potent influence, working on children, teachers, parents and public opinion.

IV Regenerating the Grades

The kindergarten is not alone in its appeal to the child and in its affiliation with the community. Traditional grade education has likewise been modified and rehabilitated until it makes an appeal to parent and child alike. In the first place, a consistent effort has been made to provide accommodations for the physical education in the grades of the fifty-seven elementary schools. Twenty-five now have fully equipped gymnasiums in which children have two or three periods of exercise each week. In the schools not so equipped the physical work is confined to calisthenics. Each year the Board of Education appropriates five hundred dollars for the Public

School Athletic League, which organizes meets and games, open to all public school pupils free of charge. Besides field days, baseball, soccer and football there is an athletic badge awarded to all pupils who pass an "efficiency" test in athletic activities.

The academic work of the grades is alive with enthusiasm. History, so often made a mass of dead names and dates, is taught in terms of life. The children learn that history is in reality a record of the things which people did, and of the forces which were at work in their lives; furthermore, that the commonplace acts of to-day will be the history of to-morrow. Translated into ideas and social changes, history stimulates thought, turning the child's mind from the purely personal side of life to the social activities of which history is made.

Arithmetic and geography begin at home, in the things which the children know and do. Both are taught in terms of child experience. Both call to the child mind the things of daily life.

English, too, which is so important an element in education, is made to reflect child experiences. Teaching the reading lesson of "Eyes and No Eyes" one teacher asked her class: "Well, children, what did you see on your way to school this morning? What did you see, Elmer?"

"Well, I saw—I saw—" and Elmer sat down.

"I saw that it had been raining in the night by the mud in the streets," said Alice; while John had seen trolley cars, and remembered that the number on one of them was 647.

A seventh grade girl had read the Psalm beginning, "Who shall ascend unto the hill of the Lord, or who shall stand in His holy place?" After asking what a psalm was, and who wrote the Psalms, the teacher asked:

"Who was David?"

"He was the king of Palestine," replied one boy promptly. After straightening out the history the teacher next asked:

"For what was David noted?"

"For being Solomon's father," ventured one little girl.

"Oh, no," protested a boy, "He was the fighter."

"Sure enough," said the teacher, "would the fact that he was a warrior naturally influence his thoughts?" After an affirmative answer from the class: "Where do we find any evidence of that in this Psalm, George?" asked the teacher.

George considered the reading a moment. "Oh, I see, it's where he says, 'The Lord mighty in battle.'"

After an elaboration of this idea the teacher went on to ask why David wrote, "Lift up your heads, oh ye gates, and the King of Glory shall come in." By careful questioning the class was led to see that cities had walls and gates; that David, who had won many victories, was accustomed to have the gates thrown wide to receive him, and that his triumphal entries had made a deep impression on his thoughts. After some more discussion the Psalm was read again, this time with surprising intelligence and feeling.

One eighth grade class in English was engaged in preparing a catalog of all of the pictures in the school, looking up the painters, their lives, their principal works, and the circumstances connected with the painting of the pictures which hung on the school wall. In the same room a girl had written a description of a sunset, in which she had said: "The western sky is illuminated with a fiery red, and the edges of the clouds are also tinted with a silvery hue."

"What would Corot say about that?" asked the teacher.

The girl thought a moment. "I guess he would say that there was too much color."

"Yes," smiled the teacher, "he would say, 'Let's go home and wait for a few moments.'"

The essay work in the upper grades is linked with all of the other school work. The children write about civics, architecture, localities, books and pictures. One girl of thirteen wrote on "The Reaper"—"As I enter my bedroom one picture especially catches my gaze. It hangs on the eastern wall. It is the picture of a large city by moonlight. The moon is bright and the stars are out. A beautiful lake borders the far end of the city, and the moon makes the lake look like a mirror. The church steeple stands out clear against the sky. It is a beautiful summer night, and while the city sleeps an angel descends and bears a little child to the heavens above. Some mother must have given up one of her beloved flowers."

No less valuable are the essays describing an ideal kitchen, a location for a house, a home, school life, and the various other things with which the child comes in contact.

Last among the academic branches, there is a carefully organized eighth grade course in civics, which, beginning with the geography and early history of Cincinnati, covers family relations and the tenement problem; the protection of public health—street cleaning, sewage, water, smoke abatement, and the activities of the Board of Health in providing for sanitation and the suppression of disease; the protection of life and property; the business life of the community—relation of the citizen to business life, the growth of commerce and industry in Cincinnati; Cincinnati as a manufacturing center, the labor problem, and the regulation of business by the government; the necessity for civic beauty; the educational forces of the community; the care of dependents and delinquents; the functions of government; and the collection and expenditure of city funds. In this way the child, before he leaves the elementary school, is given an idea of the real meaning of citizenship.

Beginning in the kindergarten, the art work extends through the high school, including in the lower elementary grades, paper-cutting and pasting related to school work, the seasons and the holidays. From the third grade on, the children make real products—trays, boxes, blotter pads, calendars, booklets and folios—work which is supplemented by object and constructive drawing and designing.

Shop-work is given to boys, and domestic science to girls, in all of the schools. The point at which these subjects are introduced and the amount of time devoted to them depends upon—what do you think? The regulations prescribed in the course of study? Not a bit of it! It depends upon the needs of the community and of the child.

Schools which are located in the poorer districts begin manual training and domestic science with the second grade, though ordinarily they are not introduced until the sixth. Normally the children are given one and one-half or two hours a week of such work, but over-age, backward and defective children may spend as much as half of their time upon it. For some of the girls a five-room flat has been rented, in which they are taught housekeeping in all of its phases. Otherwise the domestic science consists of hand and machine sewing, the designing and making of simple garments, the planning and preparation of food, and the organization and care of a household. Wherever possible, the boys make useful products in their shop-work, instead of constructing show pieces which have no value.

From top to bottom the grades are shaped to meet the needs of children. Each class and each school is built around this central idea. The school system, instead of taking the usual form of a cumbrous machine, is a delicate mechanism adjusted to the wants of Cincinnati children.

V Popularizing High School Education

Not content with making the grades interesting, the school authorities of Cincinnati have made the high schools so profitable and popular that ninety-five out of each one hundred children who complete the eighth grade go to the Cincinnati high schools. Furthermore, during the past six years the high school attendance in Cincinnati has doubled. These two noteworthy conditions are the product of carefully matured and efficiently executed plans, and of infinite labor. Yet the results have more than repaid the labor which they cost.

"Our first task," explained Dr. E. D. Lyon, principal of the Hughes High School, "was to persuade the community that it needed high school training. Next we secured two fine new high school buildings. Then those of us who are engaged in high school work faced the supreme task. We had to prove to the people that their expenditures on high schools were worth while, by providing a high school education that would mean something to the pupils and to the community." Note the spirit of social obligation—a feeling prevalent throughout the Cincinnati schools.

"Most parents fail to see the importance of the high school problem," said Assistant Superintendent Roberts, "because they never make consistent efforts to have their children choose their vocations intelligently. We began our work right there, at the bottom, by telling the parents of grade children about the high school courses, and what they meant. Eighth grade teachers, under the guidance of Mr. F. P. Goodwin, are expected to talk to their classes regularly on the vocational opportunities in Cincinnati and elsewhere, and to help the children get started right in high school careers. Besides that, we take the grade children on trips to the high schools, showing them on each trip some striking feature of high school work. Parents' meetings are held, in which the high schools are explained and discussed, and we send circulars to the parents of sixth, seventh and eighth grade pupils, explaining the high school work as simply as may be."

After arousing such expectations, the high school cannot fulfill its obligations in any way other than by the provision of a thorough course of study adapted to the needs of all types of pupils. The preparation for this in Cincinnati has been made with consummate skill. The pupil, on entering the high school, may select any one of the nine general courses, in which there are twenty-three possible combinations of subjects.

Four of the courses—General, Classical, Domestic Science and Manual Training—prepare for various colleges and technical schools. The other five courses—Commercial, Technical Co-operative Course for Boys; Technical Co-operative Course for Girls; Art and Music, lead to vocations. Housed in the same high school building is this range of work, which permits boys and girls to select a course which will bear directly on almost any line of work that they may care to follow in later life.

Each course is shaped to give the children who select it a definite training in the line of their interest. The General Course prepares pupils for college; the Domestic Science Course shows girls how to make and keep a home; the Commercial Course turns out bookkeepers; the Technical Co-operative Courses, enabling boys and girls to spend part of their time in the school and part in the factory, are arranged in co-operation with the principal industries of Cincinnati. The Art and Music Courses, like the other special work, are in the hands of experts who are competent to give a practical direction to the activity of their pupils.

In passing, it is interesting to note that the people of Cincinnati are getting the best possible use out of their splendid high school equipment. In addition to the regular classes which fill the Woodward High School from 8:30 to 3:00, the pupils in the continuation courses occupy the building every afternoon and all day Saturday. Five nights a week it is filled by an enthusiastic night school, three thousand strong, and during six weeks of the summer vacation a summer school holds its sessions there. It would be difficult to find a school plant which comes nearer to being used one hundred per cent of its time. To be sure, such things were not done "in father's time," but then the people of Cincinnati have a theory that while a good thing is worth all it costs, it does not pay to let even the best of things decay for lack of use. That is why the school system tingles from end to end with vigor and enthusiasm.

VI A City University

Besides the kindergarten, elementary schools, and high schools, the city of Cincinnati has a university, which, like all of the other educational forces of the city, is tied up with the general educational program. Those graduates of the Cincinnati high schools who desire to go to college, may pass from the high school of Cincinnati into the University of Cincinnati without a break in the continuity of their education.

The University of Cincinnati is a municipal university. The city appropriates one-half of one mill on the general assessment, for university purposes. The board of education appropriates ten thousand dollars a year toward the maintenance of the Teachers' College, the school in which the city teachers are trained. The training school for kindergarteners is affiliated with the university, having the same entrance requirements as the other university courses. In explanation of this close connection between the city and the university, President Dabney begins his 1911 report to the board of directors by saying: "An effort has been made in this report to explain the service of the university to the city and people of Cincinnati. It is therefore not only an official report to the directors, but is also a statement for the information of all citizens." Begun in this spirit of public obligation, the report details the services of the Teachers' College in supplying teachers; of the School of Economics and Political Science in supplying municipal experts; and of the Engineering School for its inauguration of the widely-known industrial co-operative courses—for be it known to the uninitiated that the five hundred students of the University Engineering School spend alternately two weeks in the school and two weeks in a shop. More than that, the Engineering School furnishes experts for municipal engineering work.

That the students of the University may feel the interest of the city in their work, preference is given to the University graduates in appointments of teachers, of municipal engineers, and of employees on such municipal work as testing food, inspecting construction, and the like. University students may thus occupy their spare time in practical municipal work.

"The University should lead the progressive thought of the community," says President Dabney, and by way of making good his proposition he avails himself of every opportunity to turn his students into municipal activities, or to co-operate in any way with the forces that are making for a greater Cincinnati.

VII Special Schools for Special Classes

There are children in Cincinnati, as in every other city, who cannot afford to go to the high school. The easiest answer to such children is, "Well, then, don't." The fairest answer is a system of schools which will enable them to secure an education even though they are at work. Cincinnati in selecting the latter course has opened a school for the education of every important group unable to attend the high schools who wish to avail themselves of advanced educational opportunities.

First there is the night school work, which, in addition to the ordinary academic courses, offers special opportunities in machine shop practice, blacksmithing, mechanical and architectural drawing, and domestic science. As these courses are carried forward in the Woodward High School building the students have all of the advantages of high school equipment.

Night school, coming after a day's exertion, is so trying that only the most robust can profit by it. No small importance therefore attaches to the operation of the compulsory continuation schools under the Ohio law, which empowers cities to compel working children between fourteen and sixteen years of age to attend school for not more than eight hours a week between the hours of 8:00 A. M. and 5:00 P. M.—hours which will presumably be subtracted from shop time. By means of this adaptation of the German system even those children who must leave school at fourteen are guaranteed school work for the next two years at least. Although this is but a minimum requirement, it represents a beginning in the right direction.

No less significant than this compulsory system are the voluntary continuation schools for those over sixteen years of age, which have been established for machinists' apprentices, for printers' apprentices, for saleswomen, and for housewives. The first two courses are conducted under the direction of a genius named Renshaw, who takes from the machine shop boys of every age, nationality and experience, fits them somewhere into his four-year course; gives them a numbered time check from his time board; teaches them reading, writing, arithmetic, mechanical drawing, geometry, algebra and trigonometry by means of an ingenious series of blueprints, which constitute their sole text-book; visits them in their shops, giving suggestions and advice about the shop work, and finally sends them out finished craftsmen, with an excellent foundation in the theoretical side of the trades. The work is entirely voluntary, yet so excellent is it that a number of Cincinnati manufacturers send their apprentices to Mr. Renshaw, paying them regular wages for the four hours of credit which the said Renshaw registers weekly on the boys' time-cards. "One firm sends sixty boys here each week," commented Mr. Renshaw's assistant. "That makes two hundred and forty hours of school work each week for which they pay regular wages. Well, sir, the superintendent there told me that they didn't so much as notice the loss."

"I tried to explain my system to one superintendent," said Mr. Renshaw, "but he wouldn't even listen. 'It makes no difference how you do it,' he grumbled, 'I don't care about that. I know that the boys are neater, more careful, more accurate, and better all-around workmen after they have been with you for a while. That's enough explanation for me.'"

Acting on such sentiments the manufacturer peremptorily dismisses the boy who does not do his school tasks satisfactorily. The responsibility is in the school, whose growing enrollment and influence tell their own story. Firms send their boys to the school with the comment that the hours of school time, for which they are paid, do not add to the cost of shop management, but do add to the value of the boys to the shop. Increased efficiency pays.

A school of salesmanship for women has met with a like success. The leading stores, glad of an opportunity to raise the standard of their employees, grant the saleswomen a half day each week, without loss of pay, during which they take the salesmanship course. The course has the hearty backing of the best Cincinnati merchants, who see in it an opportunity, as Mr. Dyer put it, "to make their employees the most skilled and intelligent, the most obliging and trustworthy, the best treated and best paid—in short, the very best type of saleswomen in the country."

That this work may keep pace with the demand for it the school authorities offer industrial instruction in any pursuit for which a class of twenty-five can be organized.

"A large number of women were born too soon to get the advantage of the courses in domestic science now being offered in our high schools," comments Mr. Dyer in his dry way. Scores of such women anxious to learn all that was known about domestic arts constituted a class for which the school was well equipped to provide. "Then suppose we give them what they need," said Mr. Dyer. Just fancy—a continuous course in domestic science! Yet there it is, in Cincinnati, with an enrollment of more than eleven hundred women, attending the public schools to learn domestic arts. What could be more rational than this Cincinnati system of making a school —even though it be a continuation school—to fit the educational needs of Cincinnati people—grown-ups and children alike?

VIII Special Schools for Special Children

The Cincinnati schools provide for special children as well as for special classes of people. First there are the unusually bright children, who "mark-time" in the ordinary classes. These children were placed in "rapidly moving classes." While omitting none of the work, they were allowed to go as fast as their mental development would allow them, instead of as slowly as the other members of the class made it necessary to move. At the beginning the teacher found these exceptionally able children lacking in effort and attention, qualities which they had not needed to keep their place in the grades. "The extra work and responsibility stimulated their mental activity, increased their power of attention, fostered thoroughness and accuracy, developed resourcefulness and initiative, and those other qualities necessary for leadership." Why should it not be so? Why should not the specially able child be taught as thoroughly as the defective one? Yet Mr. Dyer, speaking from experience, remarks: "Strange to say, it is harder to establish such classes than defective and retarded ones." Strange indeed!

For the sub-normal or retarded children Cincinnati has made ample provision. Spending from a quarter to a half of their time in manual work, the children are no longer tortured with the doing of things beyond their powers. The overgrown boys have instruction in shop work. The overgrown girls have a furnished flat in which they learn the arts of home-making at first hand. There are in all over four hundred children in these schools.

Similar accommodations are provided for other special groups. The anaemic and tubercular children are taught in two open-air schools; six teachers are detailed to instruct the deaf children; one teacher devotes her time to the blind children, and ten teachers are employed to take charge of those children who are mentally defective. Thus, by adjusting the schools to the needs of special groups of people, and of special individuals, Cincinnati is providing an education which reaches the individual members of the community.

IX Playground and Summer Schools

The vacation school is planned to meet the needs of the children in the crowded districts during the hot summer months. "For that reason," says Mr. Dyer, "it provides industrial work of all kinds unassociated with book instruction, but mingled with a great amount of recreational activity—excursions, stories, folk-dancing, and a wide variety of games."

The field of industrial activity is a broad one, including cooking, nursing, housekeeping, sewing, knitting, crocheting, weaving and basketry; drawing and color work, brush and plastic work; bench work with tools, making useful articles; sports and games, including folk-dancing for girls and ball for boys. The primary and kindergarten classes offer a delightful round of song, story, games, excursions, paper work and other forms of construction.

For the girls who have to take care of babies there are special classes. The boys make useful articles in the shops, and the girls, in sewing-room and cooking laboratory, learn to do the things around which the interests of the home always center. By co-operation with the park commissioners, the playgrounds were made an integral part of the summer school work.

Besides the recreational summer school Cincinnati has maintained for the past five years an academic summer school, in which children might make up back work in school, or do special work in any line which was of particular interest to them. In these schools "the very best instructors that can be secured" are employed, and their recommendations are accepted by the school principals when the fall term opens. "This school is one of the means taken to deal with the problem of repeaters in our schools," says Mr. Dyer. "Instead of requiring children who are behind to fall back a year, they may, if they are not hopeless failures, but only deficient in a few studies, remove their deficiencies in the summer school and go on with their class. We have followed up these pupils," Mr. Dyer adds, "and found that a normal percentage keep up with the class in succeeding years."

X Mr. Dyer and the Men Who Stood With Him

A spirit of comradeship and hearty co-operation breathes from every nook and cranny of the Cincinnati schools. Principals and teachers alike sense the fact. Alike they aim toward the upbuilding of the schools.

"Never in my life have I found such a spirit of mutual helpfulness," says Assistant Superintendent Roberts. "Every teacher has felt that she had a part to play, that she counted, that her suggestions were worth while, and she has worked earnestly toward this end."

"Everywhere I encounter the same willingness to co-operate with the schools," said Superintendent Condon, after spending three months in the place that Mr. Dyer vacated when he became superintendent of the Boston schools. "There is a heartiness in it, too, that grips a man."

"There is always the jolliest good-fellowship in the Schoolman's Club," exclaimed a grammar school principal. "It's always 'Roberts' and 'Lyon' and 'Dyer' there. They're as good as the rest, no better. We all go there to work, and to work hard for the schools."

On such a spirit is the school system of Cincinnati founded. From its point of vantage, set upon its high hill of ministry to child needs, it flashes like a searchlight through the storm of nineteenth century pedagogical obscurity. The optimist sings a new, glad song; the pessimist is confounded; the searcher after educational truth uncovers reverently before this masterpiece of educational organization, this practical demonstration of the wonders that may be accomplished where head and heart work together through the schools, for the children.

Such is the triumph, but whose the glory?

"It is not mine," protests Mr. Dyer, "I did only my part." "Nor mine," "Nor mine," echo his assistants. Truly, wisely, bravely spoken. The glory is not to Mr. Dyer, nor to any other one man or woman—the glory is to Mr. Dyer and the men and women who worked with him for the Cincinnati schools.

"My predecessor was an able organizer," explained Mr. Dyer. "He left things in splendid condition, and we took up his work. There were five things which marked great epochs in the upbuilding of the Cincinnati schools:

"First, we established the merit system for the appointment of teachers.

"Second, we improved the school buildings and equipment.

"Third, we organized special courses for children who were not able to profit by the regular work.

"Fourth, by putting applied work in the grades we gave the children a chance to use their hands as well as their heads.

"Fifth, we enlarged the school system by adding buildings and courses until there was a place in the schools for every boy and girl, man and woman in Cincinnati who wanted an education.

"That was the sum total of our work. It was a long and difficult task." Mr. Dyer's tall form straightened a trifle. His earnest, determined face relaxed. From under his bushy eyebrows flashed a gleam of triumph—the triumph of a strong, purposeful, successful man. "But when it was all over," he concluded, "and when the things for which we had striven were accomplished we knew that they were worth while."

When Mr. Dyer left his position in Cincinnati to become Superintendent of the Boston schools, there was, on every hand, a feeling of loss and of uncertainty among those most interested in the city's educational problems. During those months which elapsed between Mr. Dyer's departure for Boston and the election of his successor there was a feeling that, after all, perhaps he was not replaceable.

Then the successor came,—a quiet man, with a constructive imagination that enabled him to grasp, readily and completely, Cincinnati's educational need. There had been an era of radical educational adjustment in the city. The school system had been changed,—artfully changed, it is true—but changed, nevertheless, in all of the essential elements of its being. Some of the changes had been made with such rapidity that their foundations had not been fully completed. The brilliant school policy which Mr. Dyer had inaugurated needed rounding out for fulfilment and completion. Randall J. Condon saw these things; and he saw, furthermore, that in a community so awakened as Cincinnati, almost any educational program was feasible, so long as it remained reasonable.

The Cincinnati school people who went to Providence for the purpose of inviting Mr. Condon to take charge of the Cincinnati schools, felt the constructive power of his leadership. Providence had been educationally transformed, and Mr. Condon was the man responsible for the transformation.

The people of Cincinnati have every cause to congratulate themselves upon the new school head. At the outset Mr. Condon said,—"I purpose, to the best of my ability, to live up to and follow out the policies inaugurated by Mr. Dyer." With the utmost fidelity he has kept his word.

There is far more in Mr. Condon's administration than a mere follow-up policy. Everywhere he is building. In the face of a difficult financial situation which compels a serious curtailment of expenses for the time being, he is insisting upon additional kindergartens, extended high school accommodations, a more intimate correlation of the elementary and high school system, and an extensive system of recreation and social centers. It is upon the latter point that Mr. Condon is laying the greatest emphasis at the outset of his administration.

The Cincinnati policy which Mr. Condon has inaugurated with regard to civic centers is admirably summed up in his statement of the case. "A larger use of the school house for social, recreational and civic purposes should be encouraged. The school house belongs to all of the people, and should be open to all the people upon equal terms,—as civic centers for the free discussion of all matters relating to local and city government, and for the non-partisan consideration of all civic questions; as recreational centers, especially for the younger members of the community, to include the use of the baths and gymnasiums for games and sports, and other physical recreations, the use of class-rooms and halls for music, dramatics, and other recreational activities, and for more distinct social purposes; as educational centers in which the more specific educational facilities and equipment may be used by classes or groups of younger or older people, in any direction which makes for increased intelligence, and for greater economic and educational efficiency; as social centers in which the community may undertake a larger social service in behalf of its members,—stations from which groups and organizations of social workers may prosecute any non-partisan and non-sectarian work for the improvement of the social and economic conditions of the neighborhood, rendering any service which may help to improve the condition of the homes, giving assistance to the needy, disseminating information, helping to employment, and in general affording the community in its organized capacity an opportunity to serve in a larger measure the needs of the individual members." Here is, indeed, a broad-gauge social school policy, to which the administrative authorities of the Cincinnati schools are fully committed.

The movement for social centers in the schools is to be under the direction of a social secretary appointed by the superintendent. Until the organization is more highly perfected, principals are free, under certain restrictions, to open their schools for classes, groups, and all other legitimate community activities.

Mr. Condon's activities in the direction of socialized school buildings finds a ready response. "There was already a large use of a number of the schools for community meetings—for welfare associations, for boys' and girls' study clubs, and for musical and social gatherings." The program is a program of extension, rather than of innovation. It has already won the approval of the citizenship.

Spontaneity must be the soul of such a movement. "It was my strong conviction that the development of such a social movement should come from the people themselves, not that a ready-made program or plan should be given them, but that they should develop their own." One by one centers are being formed. The Board of Education furnishes the building, the local social center organization pays the immediate expenses which its activities incur. The movement has been started right. "I am a great believer in democracy," Mr. Condon says. "The people can be trusted to settle social questions as they should be settled, provided all sides can be fully presented and time taken for deliberation. The school house affords the one opportunity where all can meet on common ground as American citizens and as good neighbors, where the question of wealth and position may be forgotten, and where what a man is in himself, and what he is willing to do for the common good, counts most."

Such is the spirit in which Mr. Dyer, the men and women who worked with him, and the men and women who succeeded him, have striven for the advancement of education; such the spirit of co-operation and progressiveism which dominates this great city school system.

FOOTNOTES:

[21] Much of this material appeared originally in Educational Foundations.

CHAPTER VIII

THE OYLER SCHOOL OF CINCINNATI

I An Experiment in Social Education

On the west side of Cincinnati, separated from the main part of the town by railroad yards, waste land and stagnant water, surrounded by factories and a myriad of little homes, stands the Oyler School. "Can any good thing come out of Nazareth?" queried a doubter. Answers, in bell tones, the philosopher, "If a man can build a better house or make a better mousetrap than his neighbor, though he fix his home in the woods, the world will find a path to his door." Because Oyler has built a better school in a better community the world sits at Oyler's feet to learn of its experiment in social education.

The first time that I went to the Oyler School I encountered a Committee of Manufacturers. A Committee of Manufacturers in a public school during business hours! These men had met to talk with the school principal over the location of a library, which the entire community had worked to secure. When the time came to go before the Park Board over in the center of the city, to secure a playground near the Oyler School, the local bank furnished automobiles, and dozens of business men, leaving their offices, took the opportunity to endorse the work of the school, and to second its demands that play space be given to West End children. The manufacturers have become interested because in less than a decade the Oyler School has changed the face of the community, creating harmony out of discord, and order out of chaos.

The struggle of Oyler is the story of a man, a delivered message, a thriving, enthusiastic school and a reborn neighborhood. Many years ago—about twenty to be exact—a young man named Voorhes was made first assistant in a West End school. Like other young men who go into school work he applied himself earnestly to his tasks, but unlike most of them he did some hard thinking at the same time. Among other things he thought about the relation between the school and the community, wondering why the two were so completely divorced from one another. Then the problem was focused on one concrete example—a boy named John, nearly sixteen years old, who had succeeded in getting only as far as the eighth grade. John, who had never taken kindly to language or grammar, began thinking pretty seriously toward the end of his last year in the grammar school. He tried, he struggled, but the syntax was too much for him. After all, it was not his fault, and he complained bitterly against a punishment in the form of "leaving down" for something which he could not help. His training was so inadequate that he was entirely unable to pass the high school examinations which, in those days, were like the laws of the Medes and the Persians.

"I am safe in saying that he did not know the difference between a verb and a preposition," said Mr. Voorhes, "but during the grammar lesson he could make a drawing of the face of the teacher that was in no sense a caricature. This phase of his ability gave me a cue to what might be done for him. Knowing both the superintendent and the principal of the Technical School, I talked the situation over with them, begging them, with all the persuasive power at my command, to take the boy, forgetting his shortcomings, and magnifying his peculiar talents, which I felt sure were considerable along mechanical lines. They acceded to my request, giving John a place in the school, to which he walked three miles back and forth daily for three years. For many years John has been superintendent of the lighting plant of a large city, and his experience has always stood out before me as a terrible rebuke to the then dominant educational regime, which could offer John nothing but a sneer. These facts took such a vital hold on me, seeming to reinforce so fully the thought that the industrial abilities which I had acquired back on the farm proved of incalculable value to me, that the resolution to promote industrial education became a fixed part of my educational creed. The memory of that lesson in educational equity kept the need for industrial training constantly in my mind, till I had opportunity to give it expression in the Oyler School."

John bespoke the needs of the community by which Oyler was surrounded. It was so different from other communities. There were the ugly straggling factory buildings, the miserable homes, their squalid tenants, and worst of all there were the rough, boisterous, over-age, uninterested, incorrigible boys and girls, who flitted from school to home, to street, to jail, and then, gripped by the infirm hand of the law, in the form of a Juvenile Court probation officer, or a truant officer, they came back to school unwillingly enough to begin the cycle all over again.

"As for discipline," remarked one of the city school officials, "the school hadn't known it for years, the probation officer couldn't keep the children in school and the Juvenile Court couldn't keep them out of jail. Even the majesty of the law is lost on children, you know." The children taunted the police; the police hated the children; the home repelled; the factory called, grimly; child labor flourished, and the school despaired.

II An Appeal for Applied Education

Such were the conditions when Mr. Voorhes became school principal. Grinding factories, wretched homes, parental ignorance, social neglect, educational impotence—few men could enter such a field of battle with a light heart, but Mr. Voorhes did.

What, think you, was his first move? He addressed to the heads of all of the factories in the neighborhood a letter, suggesting the establishment of a manual training department in connection with the grade work of the Oyler School. "As I become more and more familiar with existing conditions in our school district," he wrote, "I am convinced that a Manual Training Department would be of vital importance to the school and to the general welfare of the community. Such departments are being looked upon to-day as necessary adjuncts to modern school equipment.

"Our school is being drained constantly of its life force by the adjacent factory demands, and if we could send pupils forth with trained hands as well as trained minds they could render a much more useful service, which, in time, would not only show itself in more profitable returns to employers, but must also tend toward a higher standard of culture in the neighborhood, and a longer continuance in school by our pupils.

"I know of no other section of the city where the actual need should make a stronger appeal for support than here. Anything you may do will be greatly appreciated."

"You can imagine my surprise," says Mr. Voorhes, "when during the next few days my mail brought me a hearty response of checks and pledges amounting to nearly a thousand dollars." Manual training was assured! No! Not yet. The Board of Education reached the conclusion that manual training in the grades was undesirable. "With the exception of $85 which I was told to use as I saw fit the checks and pledges were alike returned to the donors. That $85 gave a piano to our kindergarten."

That failure back in 1903 was the seed-ground of later success. The community was interested to the extent of a thousand dollars at least. The manufacturers were not only interested in education, but were willing to support it financially. There was a change of administration. Mr. F. B. Dyer became Superintendent of Schools and at once met the situation by establishing a manual training center in the Oyler School.

III Solving a Local Problem

The end was not yet, however. The truant officers and the Juvenile Court were still busy keeping Oyler children out of mischief and in school. The conventional type of manual training—one period per week in the sixth, seventh and eighth grades—was not holding the pupils.

"The children were not getting enough manual work to establish either habit or efficiency," Mr. Voorhes comments, "besides, this work reached only to the sixth grade. At this time there were in the school fifty boys and girls below the fifth grade who were from two to five years behind their normal classes. That is to say, they were—most of them—of that unfortunate class that has seen more trouble in a few years than most of us see in a lifetime. I was constantly asking myself: 'Where do these folks come in?' 'What is our school doing to help their function in life?' 'Are we really of any assistance to them after all?' 'Is it worth their while to come to our school?' My sympathy for the pupils was constantly growing, and I went at last in desperation to the superintendent with a plan for a revolution in the organization of my school, a revolution that I was sure would meet the needs of the community and one upon which I was willing to stake my reputation if I had any."

At this point it is worth remembering, parenthetically, that Cincinnati school men have a habit of going about their school problems in very much that spirit, beginning by sizing up the needs of the community, continuing by becoming imbued with an idea of the community needs and ending by presenting this idea to the school authorities and getting—within bounds—carte blanche to make their schools serve the locality in which they are situated.

This was Mr. Voorhes's experience. He was told to go ahead and make good—a permission of which he availed himself in an astoundingly short space of time by introducing a system of applied education, aimed to meet the needs of the children who attended the Oyler School.

"There is a peculiar situation," said Mr. Dyer, "and it needs peculiar handling. You have only one problem to solve—that of the west end. Go ahead!" Mr. Voorhes did go ahead with a plan under which all children in the sixth and seventh grades were given three periods a week in laboratories and shops. Subnormal pupils in the third, fourth and fifth grades were to have four and one-half hours (one school day) for applied work each week. In order to give special help to backward pupils they were sent in small groups to the seventh and eighth grade teachers while their classes were doing applied work. Below-grade children go to the eighth grade teacher for special work in arithmetic and geography, and the seventh grade teacher for English and history. In this way the backward children from the lower grades have special training by the best equipped teachers in the school.

The eighth grade pupils give one-fifth of their time to applied work. During the year the boys have, in addition to the shop-work, twenty lessons in preparing and cooking plain, substantial meals. To make this "siss" work palatable to the sterner sex much of it takes the form of instruction in camp life—cooking in tin cans and other handy home-made devices. In a community where boys have always been trained to regard home work as menial, but where the absence of servants makes a "lift" from the husband or brother such a Godsend to the wife at odd times, the value of giving grade boys a taste for cooking can hardly be over-estimated.

The boys also receive twenty lessons in the simpler forms of sewing—darning, hemming, sewing on buttons. At the same time the girls are taught the use of simple tools.

IV Domestic Science Which Domesticates

Beginning with the second grade the girls have domestic science while the boys are at manual training. This domestic science has a truer ring to it than most of the teaching which passes under that name. The children at Oyler have a peculiar need for domestic science, because in many of the homes mother works out, and even when she is not away her knowledge of domestic arts is so rudimentary that she can impart little to her daughters. So it comes about that the Oyler School seeks to teach the girls all that they would have under intelligent direction in a normal home.

Once each week they cook and once they sew, devoting from one-eighth to one-fifth of their entire time to these activities. By way of preparation for both cooking and sewing they are carefully trained in buying. They must make the dollar go a long way—buying in season the things cheapest at that time and preparing them in a way to yield the maximum of return. For example, they are called upon in January to buy a 50 cent dinner for six persons. Laura Wickersham's cost list is:

Soup meat	$0.20
Can of tomatoes	.10
Spaghetti	.05
Cheese	.05
Bread	.05
Butter, etc.	.08
	$0.53

Gus Potts, a mere boy, makes this suggestion:

Meat	$0.20
Potatoes	.05

Cabbage	.05
Bread	.05
Milk	.04
Butter	.05
Coffee	.05
	$0.49

In their cooking laboratory they learn to cook simple foods, one thing at a time, until they reach the upper grades, where they must prepare entire meals on limited allowances.

The sewing is equally practical. The girls learn to patch, darn, hem and make underclothing and dresses. Then, going into homes where no intelligent needlework has ever been done—where frequently a darning needle is unknown—they teach the mother and older sisters how to sew, until whole families, under the influence of one school child, improve their wardrobe and reduce their cost for clothing. Certain sewing days in school, called darning days, are sacred to the renovation of worn-out garments which the girls bring from home.

The Oyler system may not turn out artists in dress design—it has no such aim. The children who come to its class-rooms are ignorant of the simplest devices known to civilization for the making of comfortable homes. The domestic science courses are organized to take care of their children by teaching them to be intelligent home-makers.

V Making Commercial Products in the Grades

No less practical is the work of the boys in the shops, since the great majority of them will enter factories. The shop-work is designed to familiarize them with the ideas underlying shop practice. Instead of making useless joints and surfaces the boys turn out finished, marketable products. The eighth grade boys, with the aid of the instructor, have built a drill-press from the scraps of machinery which were found lying about. Now they are at work on an engine. Elaborate products you will say, for eighth grade boys, yet these boys are likely interested, they do their task with zest, and linger about the shop after school hours are over—anxious to complete the jobs which the day's work has begun.

Boys in grades two to six made three dozen hammer handles for use in the high school machine shops. Of forty-two pieces of rough stock there were produced thirty-six handles, a record which some commercial shops might envy. These same boys made a book and magazine rack, of rather elaborate design, and an umbrella rack for each of the schools in Cincinnati. These racks, displayed in the offices of the various principals, would stand comparison with a high grade factory product. The boys are now engaged in making a desk book-rack (a scroll saw exercise) for every school teacher in Cincinnati. When they have finished there will be more than a thousand.

Besides these routine class exercises the Oyler boys are privileged to make anything which appeals to them and for which they can supply the material. The school machines are theirs, subject to their use at any time. Taking advantage of this, the boys sharpen the home knives and hatchets, make axe handles, umbrella racks, hall stands, stools, sleds, cane chairs, and repair or make any product which fancy or home necessity may dictate.

VI A Real Interest in School

Let no one infer that the academic branches are neglected at Oyler. Far from it, they are taught with consummate skill by a corps of teachers who enjoy the work because they find the children interested. Strange to relate, an interest in school came in at the front door with Mr. Voorhes' new plan for applied education. The wild boys and dishevelled girls of the West End, who had erstwhile hated school, came now to participate in school activities with an interest seldom surpassed in public or private schools.

"You see," Mr. Voorhes remarked, "a day a week in the shop or laboratories is just about enough to keep down the high spirits of the older ones, and at the same time give them an applied education of which they feel the value. That one day of practical work did the trick. It made the other four days of academic work taste just as good as pie."

Mr. Voorhes' plan arrived. It won the interest of the children and later with the assistance of the Mothers' Club and the kindergarten it won the sympathy of the community.

VII The Mothers' Club

Like all of the other school centers in Cincinnati, Oyler has a kindergarten and a Mothers' Club, around which the change in community feeling has centered, until Mr. Voorhes describes them as "the most important influence that ever came into our school." Yet the kindergarten here, as elsewhere, has had a life and death grapple for existence. In the West End, dominated by its conservative, German atmosphere, the pleas for kindergartens fell on deaf ears. At last, after much preparation, a meeting of mothers and children was held for the purpose of forming an organization; at the meeting there were thirteen children and five mothers, and all antagonistic, or at best suspicious.

"I went around and played with every one of those children," said Mr. Voorhes, "talking to the mothers, and trying to persuade them that this was not failure, but merely the forerunner of success. The next day I went into every grade, saying to the children:

"'What was the matter? Mother did not come to the Mothers' Meeting yesterday.'

"'Oh, she couldn't leave the baby.'

"'Leave the baby! Why, of course not. No one expected her to leave the baby. Tell her to come and bring the baby along.'"

So another meeting was held, and another to which the babies were brought —some women bringing as many as three, who were too young to go to school. At one Mothers' Meeting, after the club had been well organized, there were twenty women, listening, discussing and nursing babies, all at once.

If the beginnings of the experiment were discouraging the results have more than offset the original disappointment. At the last meeting (in January) seventy of the eighty-five paid up members were present, intelligent, eager, interested, participating heartily in the discussions. It has cost years of labor, but these mothers have reached the point where they can talk intelligently about the children and their needs.

"Only yesterday," said Miss Phelps, Kindergarten Director, "one mother said to me: 'I used to be the most impatient woman with my children—I simply couldn't stand it when they refused to do what I told them. The other day my mother said to me, "You're about the most patient woman I ever saw. What's done it?" And I said to her: "Well, mother, I do not know of anything except those folks at the kindergarten, which all helped me to look at children in a very different way."'"

Through the Mothers' Meetings the mothers have come to feel that they are co-operating with the teacher and the school. Those mothers who have children in the upper grades as well as in the kindergarten go to the grade teachers too, seeking advice, or making suggestions. They have learned to feel that they are an essential part of the educational plan, and their enthusiastic interest tells of the advantages gained by this co-operation.

The Oyler Mothers' Club has been the center of the movement to clear up the community. Through them and through the grades refuse has been cleaned and kept from the streets. The club maintains, out of its fund, a medicine chest at the school, which is used by the visiting nurse. It has cleaned up the children, and that is no small item.

"Back in 1904," says Mr. Voorhes, "I had five hundred of the children vaccinated in my office, and such dirt and vermin I never saw! Nearly every child had the high water mark on his wrist, and their clothes and bodies were filthy. They didn't know a bathtub from a horse trough; they don't now for the matter of that, because there are scarcely a dozen houses in this section that have bathtubs, but the children are clean."

Each year the old members of the Mothers' Club bring in the new mothers, saying to Miss Phelps: "This is my mother, I brought her," "This is mine!" with a delighted satisfaction in having added something to the club. The kindergarten, filling two rooms, is thriving, and the kindergarten teachers, visiting and advising in the home, are cordially welcomed everywhere.

VIII The Disappearance of "Discipline"

"Discipline," smiled Mr. Voorhes, "no, we don't mention the word any more. Five years ago the discipline problem in this school was more serious than in any school in town. We couldn't handle it, not even with a club. To-day the discipline looks after itself."

The disciplining of an undisciplined school may sound like an immensely difficult task. Wrongly essayed it would be. Rightly directed it becomes the merest child's play. The teachers have disciplined the school—disciplined it through kindness—and here, again, the inspiration may be traced to the Mothers' Club and the kindergarten, for it was in the kindergarten that the first real attempt was made to bring this school into closer relations with the home by home visiting. Little by little the example told on the grade teachers, who went to see the children when they were absent; nor was it long before a custom grew up in the school, by virtue of which a teacher who wished to visit one absent child, might pick her own time to make her visit. If perchance the psychological moment was during school hours, she went then, while another teacher or the principal took her place.

Among the many illustrations of the efficiency of this system one stands out strongly. A boy had been away for a week, sick with rheumatism, when his teacher decided to call and see him. She went hesitatingly, however, for this boy had been rough and troublesome all through school, but particularly to her. At last her mind was made up. She visited the boy and came away radiant, overjoyed at the cordial reception he had given her. Again she went, and the mother, opening the door with a glad face, said:

"Come right in, Tom's been looking for you."

"Is he better?" the teacher asked.

"Yes, pretty much, but he said that he would get well right quick when you came to see him again."

Does anyone wonder that the boy should feel so kindly over attentions to which he was not accustomed? Is it strange that he should have come back to school with a firm resolve to be decent to his teacher?

Discipline? There is no longer a problem of discipline. The teachers are enthusiastic over the work, because they can see its results in the changed homes and lives about them. The children engaged in occupations which they enjoy and sensing the efforts of the school in their behalf, discipline themselves by being frank and hearty in work or in play.

Mr. Voorhes is not surprised at this transformation. The plan on which he staked his reputation was a simple one, based on the idea of serving a community which he had studied carefully, by providing for it an education that met its needs. Though revolutionary from an educational viewpoint, the plan succeeded because it was socially sound—because it linked together the school and the community, of which the school is a logical part.

IX The Spirit of Oyler

Oyler has a motto, a very shibboleth, "The school for the community and the community for the school." Not only do its principal and teachers believe that the school must center its activities about the needs of the community in which it is located, but they put their belief into practice, studying the community diligently and seeking to find an answer for every need which it manifests. Out of this spirit of service has grown up a warmth of feeling and interest among the teachers seldom surpassed anywhere.

"When I came to Oyler I felt about it as Sherman felt about war," says Mr. Voorhes. "Now I would not trade places with any school man in Cincinnati. The teachers feel the same way. Never yet have we had a teacher who wanted to leave. Each one has her class, that is enough. We have no problem of discipline now. The children and their parents are working for the school.["]

Sometimes people get the idea that Mr. Voorhes does not do very much. One visitor spent half a day observing, and then sitting down in his office she said:

"Mr. Voorhes, I have been here half a day and I haven't seen you around at all. What do you do?"

"Madam," answered Mr. Voorhes, "I am a man of leisure. All I do is to sit here at this desk, ready to get behind any one of my teachers, with two hundred and fifty pounds from the shoulder, in order to prevent anybody or anything from getting in the way of her work."

Small wonder that the teachers like to stay. Small wonder that the work which the school does commands the respect of the people of Cincinnati. In the school, as well as in the neighborhood, each person has a task and a fair chance to do it well.

From its position as "the worst school in Cincinnati" Oyler has risen, first in its own esteem, and then in the esteem of the city, until it is looked upon everywhere as a factor in the life of the west end, and an invaluable cog in the educational machinery of the city. Its tone has changed, too. Mr. Roberts, who came, a total stranger, to assist in the work while Mr. Voorhes was sick, says, "I have never heard a word of discourtesy or a bit of rudeness since I came to this school." That is strong testimony for a new man in a new place. Splendidly done, Oyler!

Mr. Voorhes has not stopped working. On the contrary, he is at it harder than ever, shaping his school to the ever-changing community needs. He has stopped disciplining, though, and he has stopped wondering about the success of his experiment. Time was when Oyler looked upon high school attendance much as a New York gunman looks at Sunday School. Last year of the thirty-three children in the eighth grade, eighteen—more than half—went to high school. The tradition against high school has been replaced by a healthy desire for more education. "One day a week in the shops," Mr. Voorhes says, "means interest and enthusiasm. Our children compete in high school with the children of grammar schools from the well-to-do sections, and with the best our boys and girls hold their own."

The community is interested. Parents and manufacturers alike come to the school, consult, advise, suggest, co-operate. The school boy is no longer sneered at by "the gang." The school has made its place in the community, and "the gang" is enthusiastically engaged in school work. The complexion of the neighborhood has changed, too. It is less rough, the police have less to do. Houses are neater, children better clothed and cared for. Oyler has won the hearts of its people, improved the food on their tables and the clothes on their backs, sent the children to high school, and their mothers to Mothers' Clubs; and the people who once uttered their profanity indiscriminately in every direction now swear by Oyler.

CHAPTER IX

VITALIZING RURAL EDUCATION

I The Call of the Country

There is a call of the land just as there is a call of the city, though the call of the city has sounded so insistently during the past century that men innumerable, heeding it, have cast in their lot with the throngs of city dwellers. Yet the city proves so unsatisfying that thousands are turning from its rows of brick houses and lines of paved streets to the fruit trees, dairy herds, market gardens and broad acres of the countryside. The call of the city is answered by a call which is becoming equally distinct—the call "Back to the Land."

The ten-acre lot may not be any nearer paradise than the "Great White Way," but there is about it a breadth of quiet wholesomeness which cannot make its presence felt in the bustle of the clanging cars and the rushing whirl of crowded streets. The unsmoked blue of the sky is over the country, as are the fragrance of flowers, woods and mown grass; the stars are brilliant by night, and by day the birds sing, and the cows and barnyard fowls talk philosophically together. The children have room to run and play between their periods of work, which is very near of kin to blessedness, because, aside from being instructive, it binds the child into the family group in a way that factory work can never do. The country cries health and enthusiasm to the world-weary soul as it does to the barefoot boy. Whittier was very near the heart of things when he wrote:

> Blessings on thee, little man,
> Barefoot boy, with cheek of tan!
> With thy turned-up pantaloons,
> And thy merry whistled tunes;
> With thy red lips, redder still
> Kissed by strawberries on the hill.

Despite the loneliness, isolation and overwork in some country places, the rural life is, on the whole, very rich in—

> Sleep that wakes in laughing day,
> Health that mocks the doctor's rules,
> Knowledge never learned of schools.

Country life holds a great promise for the future—a promise of vigorous manhood and womanhood, and of earnest, sane living. Through the rapidly progressing country school, more perhaps than through any other agency, this promise may be fulfilled. There are two possibilities in the development of the country school. On the one hand, several one-room schools may be consolidated into one central graded school, to which the children are transported at public expense; on the other hand, the old-time, one-room school may be reorganized and vitalized.

II Making Bricks with Straw

Even the doughtiest son of the soil must needs admit that the farmer of the past, living secluded in his house or village, was provincial, narrow, bigoted and individualistic. Times are rapidly changing, however, and out of the old desolation of rural individualism there is arising the spirit of wholesome, virile co-operation, which has transformed the face of many a country district almost in the twinkling of an eye. Nowhere is this co-operative spirit better expressed than in the consolidated country schools, which are organized, like the city school, by subjects and grades.

Considered from any viewpoint, the consolidated school is superior, as a form of organization, to the district school. Rather, the consolidated school permits organization, and the district school does not. Wherever it has been tried the testimony in favor of consolidation is overwhelming.

"Comparison," cried one county superintendent in consternation. "Comparison! There is no comparison. The old one-room school, like the one-horse plough, has seen its day. The farmers in this country, after figuring it out, have reached the conclusion that the one-room school is in the same class with a lot of other old-fashioned machinery—good in its day, but not good enough for them. That is why over eighty per cent of our schools have been consolidated. You see it's this way: The farmers need labor badly, and rather than see their sons go to a school where they are called on once or twice a day by a sadly overworked teacher they would put them to work on the farm. The consolidated school wins them with its good course of study and the boys stay in school."

That is the first, and perhaps the most vital, advantage of the consolidated school—it permits the enlargement of the course of study. Sewing, cooking, agriculture, manual training, drawing and music, have all been introduced, because the teachers have time for them. High school work has been added, too. The consolidated school, in so far as the course of study is concerned, is very nearly on a par with the graded school of the city.

Have you ever attended a one-room country school? If you have not you can form but the faintest idea of what it means to the teacher. Her day is so split up with little periods of class work that she can never do anything thoroughly. Here, for example, is an average schedule of work for a one-room class in Indiana:

DAILY PROGRAM

FORENOON

Time	Class	Grade
8:30	Opening Exercises	All
8:40	Reading	Primary
8:45	Reading	First
8:50	Reading	Second
8:55	Reading	Third
9:00	Reading	Sixth
9:10	Grammar	Fourth
9:20	Grammar	Fifth
9:30	Grammar	Sixth
9:40	Grammar	Seventh
9:50	Grammar	Eighth
10:00	Reading	Fourth
10:10	Reading	Seventh
10:20	Recess	All

10:30	Reading	Primary
10:40	Reading	First
10:50	Numbers	Second
11:00	Numbers	Third
11:05	Arithmetic	Fourth
11:15	Arithmetic	Fifth
11:25	Arithmetic	Seventh
11:35	Arithmetic	Eighth
11:50	Reading	Fifth
Noon	Noon	All

Appalling, do you say? What other word describes it adequately? There are twenty-one teaching periods in the morning; twenty-four in the afternoon. Forty-five times each day that teacher must call up and teach a new class. The college professor is "overloaded" with fourteen classes a week. This woman had two hundred and twenty-five. Will any one be so absurd as to suppose that she can do them or herself justice?

Consolidation, among its many advantages, reduces the number of classes per day, and increases the time which the teacher may devote to each class. Note the contrast between that schedule of a one-room teacher and the teaching schedule of a consolidated school teacher in the same county:

Teacher's Daily Program

FORENOON

Time	Class	Grade
8:30	Opening Exercises	All
8:45	Desk	1-B
8:50	Phonetics	1-A
9:00	Phonetics	1-B
9:15	Reading	1-A
9:30	Reading	Second

9:45	Rest Exercise	All
10:00	Nature	All
10:15	Rest	All
10:30	Words	1-B
10:50	Words	1-A
11:10	Numbers	Second
11:30	History	1-A

The "district," or one-room, schools in Montgomery County, Indiana, have twenty-three pupils per teacher, scattered over six grades. The consolidated schools in the same county show sixteen pupils per teacher, in three grades. While the teacher in the district school averages twenty-seven recitations a day, the teacher in the consolidated school has eleven; but the time per recitation is: district, thirteen minutes; consolidated, twenty-nine minutes. The number of minutes which the district teacher may give to each grade is fifty minutes; the consolidated teacher has one hundred and seventeen minutes per grade. Badly sprinkled with figures as that statement is, it gives some idea of the increased opportunities for effective teaching in the consolidated school. No teacher can do justice to twenty-seven classes per day, and an average recitation period of thirteen minutes is so short as to be almost unworthy of mention.

Most consolidated schools, in addition to the ordinary rooms, have an assembly room in which lectures, festivals, socials, public meetings, and farmers' institutes are held. Acting as a center for community life, the consolidated school takes a real place in the instruction of the community. The big brick or stone building, well constructed and surrounded, as it usually is, by well-kept grounds, furnishes the same kind of local monument that the court house supplies in the county seat. People point proudly to it as "their" public building. It is an experience of note in traveling across an open farming country to come suddenly upon a splendidly-equipped, two-story school, set down, at a point of vantage, several miles away from the nearest railroad.

The consolidated school at Linden, Montgomery County, Indiana, for example, situated in a town of scarcely three hundred inhabitants, is equipped with gas from its own gas-plant; with steam heat; ample toilet accommodations; an assembly room; and halls so broad that the primary children may play some of their games there in bad weather.

One of the most widely discussed among consolidated schools is the John Swaney Consolidated School, of Putnam County, Illinois.[22] The John Swaney School occupies a twenty-four acre campus, lying a mile and a half from the nearest village, and ten miles from the nearest town. The agitation for consolidation in Putnam County led John Swaney and his wife to give twenty-four acres as a campus for a local consolidated school. Hence the name and much of the success which has attended the work of the school.

The school cost $15,000, equipped. It is of brick with four class-rooms, two laboratories, a library, offices, a manual training shop, a domestic science kitchen, and a basement play-room. The building is lighted, heated, and ventilated in the most modern fashion. The John Swaney School thus came into existence with an equipment adequate for any school and elaborate for a school situated far from the channels of trade and industry.

The course of study organized includes all of the modern specialized work which the effective city school is able to do. Securing good teachers and possessing unique facilities, the school carries boys and girls through a series of years, in which intellectual, experimental, manual, recreational, and social activities combine to make the school the center of community life and community influence.

The school campus is used as a laboratory and a play ground. The trees provide subject matter for a course in horticulture. The fertile land is turned to agricultural use, and the broad expanse of twenty-four acres furnishes additional space for games and sports.

The social life of this school is no less effective than is its location and equipment. The teachers' cottage, an old school building converted for this purpose, furnishes a center for the life of the teaching staff, and makes a background for the social life of the entire school. There are two strong literary societies, including all of the pupils in the school. Each year plays are presented on the school stage. There are musical organizations, parents' conferences, entertainments, and community gatherings of all descriptions. In every sense, the John Swaney School is a community center.

Prosperity has followed in the wake of this educational development. The John Swaney School is known far and wide, and consequently farm renters and farm buyers alike seek the locality because of the educational opportunities which the school affords for their children, and because of the social opportunities which the community around the school affords for them.

The movement for school consolidation, like many another good movement, originated in Massachusetts. From that state it has spread extensively to Indiana, Minnesota, Iowa, Kansas, Idaho, Washington, and a number of other states,—East, West, and South. In every progressive rural community, wherever prosperous farmers and comfortable farm homes are found, there the consolidation movement is being discussed, agitated, or operated.

The movement toward consolidation has been particularly active during the past few years in the South. The Southern States are, for the most part, largely agricultural communities. The rural population far outnumbers the urban population, and it is in these districts, therefore, that the consolidated school can have its greatest influence. By 1912, the state of Louisiana alone was able to report over 250 consolidated county schools. Georgia, Florida, and North Carolina show themselves almost equally active in forwarding this generally accepted progressive educational movement.

The difficulties involved in consolidation may be summed up under two heads. There is, first of all, the conservatism and prejudice of those people who believe that the things which were good enough for their fathers, are still good enough for them. Secondly, there are the technical difficulties involved in transporting pupils from distant localities to the school center. Roads are bad at certain times of the year. Wagons are costly. Desirable drivers are difficult to secure. These factors, taken together, make the administrative difficulties of the consolidated school far greater than those of the old-time one-room country school.

The forces operating to overcome these difficulties are destined ultimately to triumph. The widespread acceptance of an agricultural education that followed upon the work of experiment stations, universities and high schools, has convinced even the most reactionary of the old-time group that there are, at least, certain things in the new generation which surpass, in their economic and social value, the like things of the old. The inroads of scientific agriculture have played havoc with agricultural tradition and conservatism. The obvious merits of the new scheme are destined to overcome the prejudices which the long continuance of the old scheme created.

The technical difficulties of transportation are being met in a number of ways. Wagon builders in various parts of the country are devoting themselves to the designing and building of wagons which will be cheap and effective. State and local authorities are actively engaged in the improvement of roads. The near future promises a standard of transportation facilities that will far surpass any that the consolidation movement has thus far enjoyed. The details of transportation administration are being worked out variously in different communities, and always with a view to the particular needs of the community involved.

While the disadvantages of consolidation lie mainly in the overcoming of prejudice and the solution of administrative problems, the advantages of consolidation seem to be primarily educational and social. The consolidated school is the only method thus far devised for giving graded school and high school privileges under adequately paid teachers to the inhabitants of rural communities. Again the consolidated school is the only method of securing a school attendance sufficiently large to provide the incentive arising from competition and emulation for pupils of each grade or age. Furthermore, the consolidated school, standing out as the most distinctive feature of a rural landscape, is readily converted into a center of rural life and activity where young folks and old folks alike find a common ground for social interests.

The advantages of the rural school are thus summed up by Mabel Carney, [23]—"For the complete and satisfying solution of the problem of rural education and for the general reconstruction and redirection of country life, the consolidated country school is the best agency thus far devised." The reasons for this statement are summed up under seven heads. In the first place, the consolidated school is a democratic, public school, directly in the hands of the people who support it. Secondly, it is at the door of farm houses and is wholly available, even more available, when public transportation is provided, than the present one-teacher school. Third, every child in the farm community is reached by it. All children may attend because of the transportation facilities afforded. Fourth, the cost of the school is reasonable. Fifth, it accommodates all grades, including the high school. The country high school, by excluding the younger children, denies modern educational facilities to any except pupils of high school grade. Sixth, it preserves a balanced course of study. While educating in terms of farm-life experience, it does not force children prematurely into any vocation, although it prepares them generally for all vocations. Lastly, the consolidated school is the best social and educational center for the rural community that has been thus far organized.

However just may be the judging of a tree by its fruit, the fruit of the consolidation movement seems uniformly good. First, because the children get to school; and second, because after they get there they are taught something worth while.

When the schools of a district are consolidated, transportation must be furnished for the students. Union Township, Montgomery County, Indiana, covering one hundred and six square miles, has replaced thirty-seven district schools with six consolidated schools. Some of the children are brought as far as five miles in wagons, or on the interurban electric cars. The wagon calls at stated hours, and the children must be ready. Tardiness is therefore reduced, until one county reports ten hundred and ninety-one cases of tardiness in its district schools (for 1910-11) and ninety-two cases in consolidated schools, although in this county there are more children in the consolidated than in the district schools.

Then, too, the children stay later in the consolidated schools. In Montgomery County, Indiana, the children who have not finished the eighth grade and who are staying away from school constitute twenty-nine per cent. of the population in the consolidated schools, as against sixty-three per cent. in the district schools. The Vernon consolidated school in Trumbull County, Ohio, has enrolled nearly nine-tenths of the children of school age. Before the consolidation only three-fifths were in school.

Theoretically, the introduction of agriculture, manual training, and other applied courses which are found in most consolidated schools, should have some effect on the lives of the children. In order to show its extent Superintendent Hall, of Montgomery County, Indiana, asked one thousand children (five hundred in district schools and five hundred in consolidated schools) what they proposed to do after they left school. Arranged according to the kind of school in which the children were, the answers showed as follows:

Chosen Profession	District Schools	Consolidated Schools
Teaching	151	122
Business	123	73
Farming	92	129
Law	55	21
Mechanics	48	86
Medicine	13	9
Ministry	12	4
Stock-breeding	3	41
Miscellaneous	3	15
Total	500	500

Agricultural studies—stock-breeding and farming—and mechanics show up strongly in the consolidated schools, at the expense of teaching, business and law in the district schools. While such figures do not prove anything, they indicate the direction in which the minds of consolidated school children are moving.

Eli M. Rapp, of Berks County, Pennsylvania, voices the spirit of the consolidation movement when he says:

"The consolidated school furnishes the framework for a well-organized, rural education. Its course of study is broader, its appeal is stronger, its service to the community more pronounced, and, best of all, it holds the children. Progressive rural communities have wakened up to the fact that unless their children are educated together there is a strong probability that they will be ignorant separately."

III Making the One-Room Country School Worth While

The brilliant success of the consolidated schools reveals the possibilities of team-work in rural education, but it cannot detract from the wonderful work which has been done, and is still being done, by the one-room rural school. Always there will be districts so sparsely settled that the consolidated school is not feasible. In such localities the one-room school, transformed as it may be by enlightened effort, must still be relied upon to provide education. Nor is this outcome undesirable. The one-room country school bristles with educational possibilities. Under intelligent direction, even its cumbersome organization may yield a plenteous harvest of useful knowledge and awakened interest.

The droning reading lesson and the sing-song multiplication table are heard no more in the progressive country school. In their place are English work, which reflects the spirit of rural things, and the arithmetic of the farm. Here is a boy of thirteen, in a one-room country school, writing an essay on "Selecting, Sowing and Testing Seed Corn," an essay amply illustrated by pen and ink drawings of growing corn, corn in the ear and individual corn kernels. Mabel Gorman asks, "Does it pay the farmer to protect the birds?" After describing the services of birds in destroying weed seeds and dangerous insects and emphasizing their beauty and cheerfulness, she concludes: "The question is, does it pay the farmer to protect the birds?" The only answer is that anything that adds to the attractiveness of the farm is worthy of cultivation. Happily a farmer who protects the birds secures a double return—increased profit from his crop and increased pleasure of living. Viola Lawson, writing on the subject, "How to Dust and Sweep," makes some pertinent comments. "I think if a house is very dirty, a carpet sweeper is not a very good thing. A broom is best, because you can't get around the corners with a sweeper." Note this hint to the school board: "We spend about one-third of our time in the school house, so it is very important to keep the dust down. The directors ought to let the school have dustless chalk. If they did there wouldn't be so much throat trouble among teachers and children. Then so many children are so careless about cleaning their feet, boys especially. They go out and curry the horses, and clean out the stables, and get their feet all nasty. Then they come to school and bring that dust into the schoolroom. Isn't that awful?" Viola is thirteen.

Over in eastern Wisconsin Miss Ellen B. McDonald, County Superintendent of Oconto County, has her children engaged in contests all the year round—growing corn, sugar beets, Alaska peas and potatoes; the boys making axe handles and the girls weaving rag carpet. During the summer Miss McDonald writes to the children who are taking part in the contests suggesting methods and urging good work. One of the letters began with the well-known lines:

> Say, how do you hoe your row, young man,
>   Say, how do you hoe your row,
> Do you hoe it fair, do you hoe it square,
>   Do you hoe it the best you know?

"How are you getting along with the contests?" continues the letter. "Are you taking good care of your beets, peas, corn or garden? Remember that it will pay you well for all the work you do upon it." In reply one girl writes: "My corn is a little over five feet high. My tomatoes have little tomatoes on, but mamma's are just beginning to blossom. My beets are growing fine. I planted them very late. My lettuce is much better than mamma's. We have been eating it right along." Mark the note of exultation over the fact that her crop is ahead of her mother's.

Sometimes the school child brings from school knowledge which materially helps his father. Here is a Wisconsin English lesson, and a proof of the saying, "Out of the mouths of babes and sucklings," all in one.

These country boys and girls take an interest in English work, because it deals with the things they know. Miss Ellen B. McDonald, County Superintendent of Schools in Oconto County, Wisconsin, publishes a column of school news in each of the three county newspapers. Here is one of her contributions, in the form of an English lesson and a counting lesson combined: (A "rag-baby tester" is a device for determining the fertility of seed corn before it is planted.)

> "My dear Miss McDonald:
>
> "The rag-baby tester is causing a whole lot of excitement. We have tested one lot and this morning started another. We notice one thing in particular, the corn which was dried by stove heat sprouts perfectly, while that dried in granaries, etc., is not sprouting at all. Last fall papa saved his seed corn, selecting it very carefully, and hung it up in the granary to dry. I selected several ears from the same field

and at the same time, and dried them on the corn tree at school. Upon testing them this spring papa's corn does not sprout at all, while mine is sprouting just exactly as good as the Golden Glow sent out to the school children. This morning I am testing some more of papa's, and if that fails he will have to buy his seed, a thing he has never had to do before. We tested the corn secured from four of our interested farmers last week and one lot germinated; the other three did not. This morning pupils from seven different homes brought seed to be tested. We had a package of last year's seed left and tested several kernels of that, as well as some sent out this year, and we think last year's seed is testing a little the better."

The new arithmetic, like the new English, deals with the country. It seems a little odd, just at first, to see boys and girls standing at the board computing potato yields, milk yields, the contents of granaries, the price of bags and the cost of barns and chicken houses; yet what more natural than that the country child should figure out his and perhaps his father's problems in the arithmetic class at school?

The geography is no less pertinent. Soil formation, drainage, the location and grouping of farm buildings, the physical characteristics of the township and of the county are matters of universal interest and concern. Every school in Berks County, Pennsylvania, is provided with a fine soil survey map of the county, made by the United States Geological Survey. What more ideal basis for rural geography?

Here and there a country school is waking up to the physical needs of country children. "Country boys are not symmetrically developed," asserts Superintendent Rapp, of Berks County. "They are flat-chested and round-shouldered." That is interesting, indeed. Mr. Rapp explains: "It is because of the character of their work, nearly all of which tends to flatten the chest. Whether or not that is the explanation, the fact remains, and with it the no less evident fact that it is the business of the school to correct the defects. In an effort to do this we have worked out a series of fifty games which the children are taught in the schools." In May a great "Field Day and Play Festival" is held, to which the entire county is invited. Each school trains and sends in its teams. Trolleys, buggies, autos and hay wagons contribute their quota, until five thousand people have gathered in an out-of-the-way spot to help the children enjoy themselves.

Mr. Rapp is a great believer in activity. Tireless himself, he has fifty teacher-farmers—men who teach in the winter and farm in the summer—an excellent setting for country boys and girls. He believes in activity for children, too. "If the school appealed as it ought to the motor energies of children, instead of having to drive them in, you would have to drive them out." To prove his point Mr. Rapp cites the instance of one man teacher, who, before the days of manual training in the schools, decided to have manual training in his one-room Berks County school.

"He did the work himself," Mr. Rapp says, "dug out the cellar and set up a shop in it. The only help he had was the help of the pupils, and the work was done in recess time and after school. They made their own tools, cabinets, book-cases, picture-frames, clock-frames, and anything else they wanted. And do you know, when it got dark, that man would send the children home from the school in order to be rid of them."

Consolidated schools help. They make rural education broader and easier, but the one-room country school, presided over by a live teacher, may be made worth while. Social events, sports, contests in farm work and domestic work, studies couched in terms of the country, may all prove potent factors in shaping the child and the community.

IV Repainting the Little Red Schoolhouse

Without, as well as within, the little red school-house may be transformed. The course of study may establish a standard in rural thought. The rural school-house may set a standard of rural architecture and landscape gardening.

How typical of old-time country schools are the lines:

> Still sits the school-house by the road,
>   A ragged beggar sunning.
> Around it still the sumacs grow,

And blackberry vines are running.

The unpainted, rough exterior of the little school vied with the unkempt school grounds. Both supplied subjects for artistic treatment. To the consternation of the poet and the romancer, the modern one-room school is painted, and the school yard, instead of being filled with a thicket of blackberry and sumac, is laid out for playground, flower-beds and gardens. The up-to-date country school, while far less picturesque, is much more architectural and more useful.

The State Superintendent of Education in Wisconsin furnishes free to local school boards plans of modern one-room schools. With a hall at each end for wraps, an improved heating and ventilating device, and all of the light coming from the north side, where there is one big window from near the floor to the ceiling, these buildings, costing from two thousand dollars up, provide in every way for the health and comfort of the children. The superintendent may go farther than to suggest in Wisconsin, however, for if a school building becomes dilapidated he may condemn it, and then state aid to local education is refused until suitable buildings are provided. The law has proved an excellent deterrent to educational parsimony.

Superintendent Kern, of Rockford, Illinois, has done particularly effective work in beautifying his schools. Within the schools are tastefully painted and decorated. Outside there are flower-beds, hedges, individual garden plots, neatly-cut grass, and all of the other necessaries for a well-kept yard. No longer crude and unsightly, the Rockford school yards are models which any one in the neighborhood may copy with infinite advantage. As the school becomes the center of community life local pride makes more and more demands. Could you visit some of the finer school buildings in Ohio, Indiana, Wisconsin and Illinois you would be better able to understand why men boast of "Our School" in the same tone that they use when boasting of their corn yields.

V A Fairyland of Rural Education

You will perhaps be somewhat skeptical—you big folks who have ceased to believe in little people—when you hear that out in western Iowa there is a county which is an educational fairyland. Yet if you had traveled up and down the country, gone into the wretched country school buildings, seen the lack-luster teaching and the indifferent scholars, which are so appallingly numerous; if you had read in the report of the investigating committee which has just completed its survey of Wisconsin rural schools the statement that in many districts the hog pens were on a better plane of efficiency than the school houses; if you had seen the miserable inadequacy of country schools North, East, South and West, and had then been transported into the midst of the school system of Page County, Iowa, you would have been sure that you had passed through the looking-glass into the queer world beyond. Yet Page County is there—a fairyland presided over by a really, truly fairy.

The schools in Page County, Iowa, which, by the way, is one of the best corn counties in Iowa, are little republics in which the children have the fun, do the work and grow up strong and kind. Each school has its song, its social gatherings, its clubs, and its teams. How you would have pricked up your ears if you had driven past the Hawley School and heard a score of lusty voices shouting the school song to the tune of "Everybody's Doing It!"

December was the time of the Page County contests, when each school sent its exhibits of dressmaking, cooking, rope-splicing, barn-planning, essay-writing and its corn-judging teams to the county seat, where they were displayed and judged very much as they would be at a county fair. Further, it was the time when the prizes were to be awarded to the boy having the best acre of alfalfa, of corn and of potatoes. (Queer, isn't it, but last year a girl got the first prize for the best crop of potatoes.) December is a great month in Page County. This year more than three thousand exhibits were sent into Clarinda, the county seat. Every boy and girl is on tip-toe with expectancy, and after the awards the successful schools are as proud as turkey cocks.

"We have never taken the thing seriously here before," explained a farmer who had left his work in mid-afternoon and come in to teach the boys of a school how to judge seed corn. "This year we're going down there to Clarinda for all that's in it." If he hadn't meant what he said he would scarcely have been spending his hours in the school-room. If the

Hawleyville boys had not been thoroughly in earnest they would not have been there, after school, learning how to judge corn.

The community around each school is agog with excitement while preparations are being made for the county contest. The men folk advise the boys regarding their corn-judging and their models of farm implements and farm buildings, while the women give lessons galore in the mysteries of country cooking, for it is no small matter to be hailed and crowned as the best fourteen-year-old cook in Page County, Iowa.

One Page County teacher conducts her domestic science work in the evening at the homes of the girls. On a given day of each week the entire class visits the home of one of the girls, prepares, cooks and eats a meal. What an opportunity to inculcate lessons in domestic economy at first hand! What a chance to show the behind-the-time housekeeper (for there are such even in Page County) how things are being done!

Because Page County is a great corn county much school time is devoted to corn. In every school hangs a string of seed corn which is brought in by the boys in the fall, dried during the winter, and in the spring tested for fertility. A Babcock milk-tester, owned by the county, circulates from school to school, enabling the children to test the productivity of their cows. Teams of boys, under the direction of the school, make their own road drags, and care for stretches of road—from one to five miles. The boys doing the best work are rewarded with substantial prizes. Do you begin to suspect the reason for the interest which the big folks take in the doings of Page County's little folks? It is because the little folks go to schools which are a vital part of the community.

Three times a year there is, in each school, a gathering of the friends and parents of the children. Sometimes they celebrate Thanksgiving, sometimes they have a "Parents' Day." Anyway, the boys decorate the school, the girls cook cake and candy, and the parents come and have a good evening. The children begin with their school song, sung, perhaps, like this Kile School song, to the tune of "Home, Sweet Home":

1. What school is the dearest,
    The neatest and best,
    What school is more pleasant,

More dear than the rest,
Whose highways and byways
Have charms from each day,
Whose roads and alfalfa,
They have come to stay.

Chorus.
Kile, Kile, our own Kile,
We love her, we'll praise her,
We'll all work for Kile.

2. Whose corn is so mellow,
Whose cane is so sweet,
Whose taters are so mellow,
Whose coal's hard to beat,
Whose Ma's and whose Grandpa's
Are brave, grand and true,
Their love for their children
They never do rue.

There follows a program like the program of any other social evening, except that very often the parents take part as well as the children. The things are interesting, too, like this little duet, sung at the Thanksgiving entertainment by two of the Kile girls:

1. If a body pays the taxes,
Surely you'll agree,
That a body earns a franchise,
Whether he or she.

Chorus.
Every man now has the ballot,
None, you know, have we,
But we have brains and we can use them,
Just as well as he.

2. If a city's just a household,
As it is, they say,

> Then every city needs housecleaning,
> Needs it right away.

> 3. Every city has its fathers,
> Honors them, I we'en,
> But every city must have mothers,
> That the house be clean.

> 4. Man now makes the laws for women,
> Kindly, too, at that,
> But they often seem as funny
> As a man-made hat.

The grand event of this fairyland comes in the summer, when the boys and girls from all of the schools go to the county seat for a summer camp, where, between attending classes and lectures, playing games and reveling in the joys of camp life, they come to have a very much broader view of the world and a more intense interest in one another.

They are only one-room schools out there in Page County, but they have adapted themselves to the needs of the community, focusing the attention of parents and children alike on the bigger things in rural life, and the ways in which a school may help a countryside to appreciate and enjoy them. So the boys and girls of Page County have their fairyland, and are devoted to the good fairy, who, in the shape of a generous, kindly county superintendent, helps them to enjoy it.

VI The Task of the Country School

The teacher of a one-room school in Berks County was quizzing a class about Columbus.

"Where was he born?" she queried.

"In Genoa."

"And where is Genoa, Ella?"

"On the Mediterranean Sea," replied Ella promptly.

"What was his business?" was her next question.

"He was a sailor," ventured a bright boy. "A sailor," chorused the class.

"Why was he a sailor, Edith?" Edith shook her head.

"Yes, George."

"Why, because he lived on the sea."

"Of course. Now think a minute. Do many of the boys from this country become sailors?"

"No'm," from the class.

"What do they become?"

"Farmers," cried the class, hissing the "f" and flattening the "a."

Certainly, the boys in a farming community, brought up on the farm, naturally become farmers, yet in the interim, between babyhood and farmer life, they go to school. How absurdly easy the task of the school—to determine that they shall be intelligent, progressive, enthusiastic, up-to-date farmers. The girls, too, marry farmers, keep farmers' homes and raise farmers' sons. How simple is the duty of seeing that they are prepared to do these things well!

The task of the city school is complex because of the vast number of businesses, professions, industrial occupations and trades which children enter. In comparison the country school has the plainest of plain sailing. What are the ingredients of successful farmers and farmers' wives? What proportion of physical education, of mental training, of technical instruction in agriculture, of suggestions for practical farm work, of dressmaking, sewing and cooking, enter into the making of farmers' boys and farmers' girls who will live up to the traditions of the American farm? To what extent must the school be a center for social activity and social enthusiasm? How shall the school make the farm and the small country town better living places for the men and women of to-morrow?

The duty of the country school is simple and clear. It must fit country children for country life. First it must know what are the needs of the country; then, manned by teachers whose training has prepared them to appreciate country problems, it will become the power that a country school ought to be in directing the thoughts and lives of the community.

FOOTNOTES:

[22] An extensive reference to this school will be found in "Country Life and the Country School," Mabel Carney, Row, Peterson & Company, Chicago, 1912.

[23] Supra, pp. 180-181.

CHAPTER X

OUT OF THE MOUTHS OF BABES AND SUCKLINGS

I Miss Belle

The sun shone mildly, though it was still late January, while the wind, which occasionally rustled the dry leaves about the fence corners, had scarcely a suggestion of winter in its soft touch. Across the white pike, and away on either side over the rolling blue grass meadows, the Kentucky landscape unfolded itself, lined with brown and white fences, and dotted with venerable trees. A buggy, drawn by a carefully-stepping bay horse, came over the knoll ahead, framing itself naturally into the beautiful landscape. Surely, that must be Joe and Miss Belle; it was so like her, since she always seemed at home everywhere, making herself a natural part of her surroundings. Another moment and there was no longer any doubt. It was Miss Belle with three youngsters crowded into her lap and beside her in the narrow buggy seat, while a dangling leg in the rear suggested an occupant of the axle.

"Well, well," cried Miss Belle, cordially, as Joe stopped, glad of any excuse not to go, "where are you bound for? You didn't come all the way over to ride back with me?"

"No, indeed, Miss Belle," I laughed back, "no one ever expects to ride with you so near the school-house. I'll walk along ahead until you begin to unload."

"Go along, now you're casting reflections on Joe's speed. Come, Joe, we'll show him." Joe, who did not leave his accustomed walk at once, finally yielded to the suggestion of a gentle blow from the whip and broke into a trot.

"Lem'me walk with you," cried the rider on the springs, slipping from her perch and stepping out beside the buggy. So we journeyed for half a mile. The horse, under constant urging, jogged along, while the spring rider and I trotted side by side over the well-made pike. Then Miss Belle drew rein in front of a small, yellow house.

"Now, out you go," she exclaimed to her young companions. "All out here but one. Goodbye, dearies. All right, up you get," and in a moment we were snugly fixed in the buggy for a half hour's ride behind Joe.

"You see those two little girls who got off there," said Miss Belle, pointing to the house we had just left, "well, they are two of a family of six—two younger than those. Their mother died last winter, so naturally I take an interest in them. Their father does his best with them, but it is a big task for a man to handle alone."

The last child was unloaded by this time, and Miss Belle, settling herself back comfortably, chatted about her work in a one-room country school in the Blue Grass belt of Kentucky.

II Going to Work Through the Children

"Maybe there are thirty-five families that my school ought to draw from," she began. "Six years ago when I took this school some of them surely did need help. Dearie me! The things they didn't know about comfort and decency would fix up a whole neighborhood for life. They wore stockings till they dropped off. Some of the girls put on sweaters in October, wore them till Christmas, washed them, and then wore them till spring. You never saw such utterly wretched homes. There was hardly a window shade in the neighborhood, nor a curtain either. It wasn't that the women didn't care—they simply didn't know.

"I saw it all," said Miss Belle, nodding her head thoughtfully, "and it worried me a great deal at first. I just had to get hold of those people and help them—I had made up my mind to that. Impatience wouldn't do, though, so I said to myself, 'Now, my dear, don't you be in any hurry. You can't do anything with the old folks, they're too proud. If you succeed at all it's got to be through the children.' So I just waited, keeping my eyes open, and teaching school all of the while, until, the first thing I knew, the way opened up—you never would guess how—it was through biscuits.["]

III Beginning on Muffins

"The folks around here never had seen anything except white bread. There wasn't a piece of cornbread or of graham anywhere. You know what their white bread is, too—heavy, sour, badly made and only half cooked. The old folks were satisfied, though, and there didn't seem to be any way to go at it except through the youngsters. Day after day I saw them take raw white biscuits and sandwiches made of salt-rising white bread out of their baskets, wondering how they could eat them. Still I didn't say anything, but every lunch time I ate corn muffins or graham wafers, with all of the gusto I could master. One day a little girl up and asked me:

"'Say, Miss Belle, what may you all be eatin'?'

"'Corn muffins,' said I. 'Ever taste them?'

"'Nope.'

"'Well, wouldn't you like a taste?'

"'Sure I would.'

"She took it, and a great big one, too. 'Um,' says she, smacking her lips, 'Um.'

"'Like it?' I asked.

"'Um,' says she again, like a baby with a full stomach.

"'Oh, Miss Belle,' piped up Annie, 'how do you make 'em?'

"That was the chance I had been waiting for.

"'Would you like to know?' I asked, and to a chorus of 'Sure,' ''Deed we would,' 'Oh, yes,' I put the recipe on the board, and it wasn't two days before those girls brought in as good corn muffins as I ever tasted. Little Annie is a good cook—never saw a better—and before the week was out she says to me:

"'Miss Belle, ma's mad with you.'

"'What all's the matter?' I asked.

"'She says since you taught us to make those corn muffins she'll be eaten out of house and home. The first night I made 'em pa ate eleven. He hasn't slackened off a bit since. He must have 'em every day.'

"That made the going pretty easy," Miss Belle went on. "The muffins were mighty good, they were new, and, by comparison, the white biscuits didn't have a show. It wasn't long before I had the whole neighborhood making corn muffins, graham wafers, black bread, graham bread and whole-wheat bread. They sure did catch on to the idea quickly. Every Monday I put a recipe on the board. These women knew how to cook the fancy things. It was the plain, simple, wholesome things that they needed to know about, so my recipes were always for them. During the week each of the children cooks the thing and brings it to me, and the one who gets the best result puts a recipe on the board Friday.

"You see, after I once got started it wasn't hard to follow up any line I liked. By the time I was putting a recipe a week on the board the mothers got naturally interested and would come to school to ask about this recipe and that. They wouldn't take any advice, you understand, not they! They knew all about cooking, so they thought, but they were mighty proud of the things their daughters did, particularly when they took the prizes at the county fair. Besides that, it made a whole lot of difference at home, because the things they made helped out a lot and tasted mighty good on the table."

Miss Belle's next move was against the cake—soggy, sticky stuff, full of butter, that was very generally eaten by all of the families that could afford it. Expensive and fearfully indigestible it made up, together with bread, almost the entire contents of most lunch baskets.

"I couldn't see quite how to go about the cake business," Miss Belle commented, "because they were particularly proud of it. Finally, though, I hit on an idea. One of the women in the neighborhood was sick. She was a good cook and knew good cooking when she saw it, so I got my sister to make an angel cake, which I took around to her. I do believe it was the first light cake she had ever tasted—anyway, she was tickled to death. It wasn't long after that before every one who could afford to do it was making angel food. Of course it's expensive, but since they were bound to make cake, that was a lot better than the other."

Similar tactics gradually replaced the fried meats by roasts and stews. When Miss Belle came, meat swam in fat while it cooked and came from the stove loaded with grease. Everybody fried meat, and when by chance they bought a roast they began by boiling all of the juice out of it before they put it in the oven. Miss Belle's stews and roasts made better eating, though. The men-folks liked them hugely and the old frying process was doomed.

"No," concluded Miss Belle, laughingly, "you can't do a thing with the old folks. Why if I was to go into a kitchen belonging to one of those women and tell her how to sift flour she would run me out quick, but when Annie comes home and makes such muffins that the man of the family eats eleven the first time, there is no way to answer back. The muffins speak for themselves."

IV Taking the Boys in Hand

While the girls were making over the diet of the neighborhood Miss Belle was working through the boys to improve the strains of corn used by the farmers, the methods of fertilizing and the quality of the truck patches. A few years ago when the farmer scorned newfangled ideas it was the boys that took home methods for numbering and testing each ear of corn to determine whether or not the kernels on it would sprout when they were planted. The farmer who turns a deaf ear to argument can offer no effective reply to a corn-tester in which only one kernel in three has sprouted. The ears are infertile, from one cause or another, and the sooner he replaces them by fertile seed the better for his corn crop.

Out beside a white limestone pike stands the school in which Miss Belle has done her work. One would hardly stop to look at it, because it differs in no way from thousands of similar country school-houses. Modest and unassuming, like Miss Belle, it holds only one feature of real interest—the faces of the children. Bright, eager, enthusiastic, they labor earnestly over their lessons in order that they may get at their "busy work," and linger over their "busy work" during recess and after school, because it glides so swiftly from their deft fingers. In this, as in everything else which she does,

Miss Belle has a system. The child whose lessons are not done, and done up to a certain grade, is not taught new stitches or new designs. Even the youngest responds to the stimulus, and the little girl in a pink frock, with pink ribbons on her brown pig-tails, lays aside the mat she is making to write "Annie Belle Lewis" on the board, and to tell you that she is seven; while John Murphy, of the mature age of eleven, stops crocheting ear-mufflers for a moment to tell you what he is doing and why he does it.

V "Busy Work" as an Asset

"You never would guess what a help the 'busy work' is," smiled Miss Belle. "You see, they never can do it until their lessons are finished, so they are as good at arithmetic as they are at patching. Then I always teach the little ones patterns and stitches where they have to count, 'One, two, three, four, five, and drop one,' you know, and in the shortest time they learn their number work. It seems to go so much more quickly when they do it in connection with some pieces that they can see. But you never would guess the best thing the sewing has done—it has stopped gossiping. It's hard to believe, I know, but it's true. There used to be a lot of trouble in this neighborhood. People told tales, there was ill feeling, and folks quarreled a great deal of the time. It wasn't long before I found out that it was the girls who did most of the tale-bearing. No wonder, either! They weren't very busy in school, and they had nothing much to do at home except to listen and talk. Really, they hadn't any decent interest in life. Of course there was no use in saying anything, but I felt that if I could get them busy at something they liked they would stop talking. It wasn't enough to start them at dressmaking, either, but when I started in on hard, fancy work designs I had them. They made pretty clothes, embroidered them; made lace and doilies. Most of the girls can pick up a new Irish-lace pattern from a fashion-book as easily as I can, and they are rabid for new patterns. The same girls who did most of the tale-bearing are busy at work, and I find them swapping patterns and recipes instead of stories."

While the girls patch, darn, crochet, hem, knit, weave baskets, make garments and do the various kinds of "busy work," the boys clean the school yard, plant walnut trees—Mrs. Faulconer, the County Superintendent, is having the school children plant nut trees along all the pikes—and do anything else which is not beneath their dignity. "They have no work benches," lamented Miss Belle, "I hope they will get them soon, although there is really no place to put them." Indeed, in a little building packed with fifty children and the school-room furniture the space is narrow.

Yet this little one-room building at Locust Grove has left such a mark on the community that when the County School Board recently decided to transfer Miss Belle to a larger school the member from her district promptly resigned, and refused to be placated until every other member of the board had apologized to him and promised to leave Miss Belle in his school.

"We never saw the old gentleman mad before," said a neighbor. "But he certainly was mad then. He had watched Miss Belle's work grow, and knew what it had meant to the children; so when they proposed to take her away he went right up in the air."

VI Marguerite

What wonder? He had seen the magic workings of a hand that felt the pulse, judged the symptoms, and prescribed a sure-to-cure remedy for a countryside full of ignorance, drunkenness, bitter hatreds and never-ending quarrels. Within a stone's throw of his house he had seen the transformation in the life of a little girl named Marguerite. Since her birth she had lived in darkness, but into her desolate home Miss Belle had sent light.

"You never saw a worse home," says Miss Belle. "Her mother was woefully ignorant of everything in the way of home-making. The children were wretchedly dressed. The house was barrenness itself—no shades, no curtains, no decorations of any kind. It was pathetic. When she came to school neither she nor her mother could sew a stitch."

Marguerite, an apt girl with her fingers, eagerly learned the needlework lessons of the school. She taught her mother to sew, while she herself made portieres and curtains, lightening up the old home with a rare new beauty.

Here again is Lillie, who is very slow at needlework and arithmetic, but who has put the family diet on a wholesome basis by learning to cook some of the most delicious, nourishing dishes. Her bread—the best in Fayette County—is light as a feather. Hannah comes back after leaving school to learn how to ply her needle. Until a year ago Christmas she could not sew a stitch; now her stitches are so neat as to be almost invisible. Mrs. Hawly, aroused to enthusiasm by her thirteen-year-old daughter, has come to school, learned plain and fancy sewing, and started to make her own and her daughter's clothes. Everywhere are the marks of a teacher's handiwork stamped indelibly on the lives of her scholars and their families. Small wonder that the old gentleman on the board was loath to part with Miss Belle!

VII Winning Over the Families

With supreme joy Miss Belle tells of her conquest of the fathers of her boys and girls—her family, as she calls it. "The children were very poorly cared for," she says. "The fathers spent the money for whiskey, and the mothers lacked the means and the knowledge to clothe the children better. Sometimes they were pitiful in their poor shoes and thin clothes. Well, sir, we got up a Christmas entertainment, and, except for one or two, the children wore the same clothes they had been coming to school in all winter —shabby, patched and dirty as some of them were. They stood up there, though, one and all, to do their turns and speak their pieces, and their fathers were ashamed. They saw their children in old clothes, and the children of some of the neighbors all fixed up, and they just couldn't stand it.

"It surely did make a difference the next year." Miss Belle's cheery face broadened with a satisfied smile. "The men didn't say a word—you know our men aren't in the habit of saying very much—but they went to town themselves the day before the entertainment and came back with new dresses for the girls and new clothes for the boys. Of course some of them were so small they would scarcely go on, while others were miles big; but every one had something new and no one felt badly.

"This Christmas," concluded Miss Belle, "our entertainment packed the school-house, and some were turned away. Just to show you how crowded it was—there were twenty-four babies there. I was ready for them, though, with two pounds of stick candy; so whenever a baby squalled he got a stick of candy quick."

Strange, good things have followed the visits of the mothers to the schools. They would never have come had it not been for the wonderful things which their children were learning with such untoward enthusiasm. One girl, who had been particularly successful with her needlework, brought her mother to school—a hard woman who had a standing quarrel with seven of her neighbors at that particular time. It took a little tact, but when the right moment arrived Miss Belle suggested that she pay a visit to a sick neighbor and offer to help. The woman went at last, found that it was a very pleasant thing on the whole to be friendly, and carried the glad tidings into her life, substituting kindness for her previous rule of incivility. To her surprise her enemies have all disappeared.

The mothers, coming to school to talk over the work of their children, have for the first time seen one another at their best. Sitting over a friendly cup of tea, chatting about Jane's dress or Willie's lessons, they have learned the art of social intercourse. Slowly the lesson has come to them, until to-day there is not a woman in the neighborhood who is not on speaking terms with every one else, a situation undreamed of five years ago.

Nine months in each year Miss Belle McCubbing holds her classes in the Locust Grove School, which stands on the Military Pike, seven miles outside of Lexington, Kentucky. "Angels watch over that school," says Mrs. Faulconer. Doubtless these angels are the good angels of the community, for in six years the bitterness of neighborhood gossip and controversy has been replaced by a spirit of neighborly helpfulness. Boys and girls, doing Miss Belle's "busy work," fathers and mothers learning from their children, have heaped upon Miss Belle's deserving head the peerless praise of a community come to itself—regenerated in thought and act, turned from the wretchedness and desolation of the past to the light and civilization of the future, saved and blessed by the lives of a teacher and her children.

CHAPTER XI

WIDE-AWAKE SLEEPY EYE

I Fitting Schools to Needs

This is the story of a school that was built to fit a town, and it begins with a hypothetical case. Suppose that there was a town—a prosperous town of some 2,247 souls, set down in the middle of a well-to-do farming district. As for business, the town has a few industries and some stores; the countryside is engaged in general farming. Suppose that the school board of such a town should come to you and say: "We are looking for a school superintendent. Are you the one?" Suppose you said, "Yes." How would you prove your point?

Out in Minnesota there is a town named Sleepy Eye, set down in a well-to-do farming district. At the head of the Sleepy Eye schools there is J. A. Cederstrom. Mr. Cederstrom has proved by a very practical demonstration that he is "the one."

When Mr. Cederstrom took charge of the Sleepy Eye schools he found an excellent school plant, an intelligent community and a school system that was like the school system of every other up-to-date two-thousand-inhabitant town in the Middle West. Before Mr. Cederstrom there lay a choice. He could continue the work exactly as it had always been carried on, improve the school machinery, and make a creditable showing at examination time. That path looked like the path of least resistance. Mr. Cederstrom did not take it, however. Instead he made up his mind that after measuring the community and the children he would, to use his own words, "fit the work to their respective needs."

"The work offered has been somewhat varied," Mr. Cederstrom explains. "I have not attempted to follow any set course or outline of work made out by some one else who is not familiar with our conditions and needs."

Where does there exist a more admirable statement of the principle underlying the new education? This man, when given charge of a school plant, deliberately chose to make the school fit the needs of the community upon which the school was dependent for support. Oblivious of tradition he set about remodeling the school in the interest of its constituency.

Sleepy Eye is located in a farming district. Many of the boys who come to the Sleepy Eye School will manage farms when they are grown men, and many of the Sleepy Eye girls will marry farmers and manage them. Here were farmer men and farmer women in the making. What more natural than to organize a Department of Agriculture?

A Department of Agriculture in a school? Yes, truly; and a short winter course for farm boys and girls who could not come the year round, and a school experiment station with school farms for the children, and a live farmers' institute that met in the school and was fed and cared for by the Department of Domestic Science, and all sorts of courses built up around the needs of the children and of the community.

II Getting the Janitor in Line

As a result of this method of course-making the school janitor found himself on the instruction staff of the school. One day a couple of the short course boys were in the engine-room while the janitor was repairing a defective pipe in the heating plant. The boys lent a hand in the work; and one of them, having a practical turn of mind, suggested that he would like to learn more about pipe-fitting in order to install a water system on the farm at home. The janitor repeated the remark to Mr. Cederstrom, who called the boys out and had a talk with them regarding the possibilities of the plan.

The outlook for the course was not bright. Every instructor in the mechanical department was working on full time. Only one way out remained and that way led to the janitor.

The janitor was a busy man during the day, but his evenings were comparatively free. After some parleying he agreed to give a course in elementary plumbing and steam-fitting on Tuesday and Thursday evenings at seven-thirty. So the boys came to school in the evening, and under the direction of the school janitor learned how to install a water system in their homes. Their work for the year consisted in making a model water system for a house, a barn and the other farm buildings. The materials for this course were picked up from the school's scrap-heap.

Perhaps some people will not understand the spirit of it—getting the janitor in line to give a course in steam-fitting from the odds and ends that are found on the scrap-heap. Such a proceeding is unconventional in the extreme. But, on the other hand, here were boys who wished to know how they might go back and improve their homes. Who shall say that the imparting of such knowledge is not the business of a real school?

III The Department of Agriculture

Let us go back for a moment to the organization of the Department of Agriculture. The school at Sleepy Eye have available what every other school should have—five acres of tillable ground. This tract at Sleepy Eye is devoted to tests and experimental work, to flower gardens and to individual school gardens—one for each child who applies.

The experimental work and tests are carried on exactly as they would be at a state experiment station. In the section of Minnesota surrounding Sleepy Eye, corn is the great staple crop. Therefore on the demonstration grounds of the Department of Agriculture, Independent School District No. 24, Sleepy Eye, Minnesota, they are growing a number of plots of corn, each plot variously planted, fertilized, cultivated, and cared for, so that the children may learn at first-hand scientific methods of discovering the best kinds of crop, and the best ways of handling a crop in their own locality.

The allotment of the school gardens carried with it instruction in engineering and in civics at the same time that the bonds between home and school were cemented. The part of the school land that was to be devoted to school gardens was turned over to the older boys, who surveyed it in exactly the same way that the United States government surveyed the homestead tracts. The plot was laid out in towns and ranges. The sections were staked and numbered. Then the children who wished to take up plots went into the newly surveyed territory, picked their plots, and filed an application with the land commissioner for a plot, stating the section, town and range. After that a line formed and the plots (20×20 feet) were allotted.

No child was permitted to take up an allotment unless he had the endorsement of a parent or guardian. The form on which this endorsement was secured was as follows:

Name_____
Grade_____
_____ Sec____ Town_____
Range_____

APPLICATION FOR LAND IN PUBLIC SCHOOL GARDEN, DEPT. OF AGR., SLEEPY EYE HIGH SCHOOL

"It is assumed that the parent or guardian who endorses this application will co-operate with the school authorities and have the applicant care for and weed said land during the growing season, and devote at least two and a half hours each week this summer to the agricultural work as may be directed or required by the Director of the Department of Agriculture, Mr. Haw.

"I hereby apply for.......... Sec.......... Town.......... Range.......... in the Public School Garden of Sleepy Eye High School, and will cultivate and care for same as may be directed by the proper authorities, and will keep a careful record of the returns therefrom and report same on or before Oct. 20, 1911. I will do the additional agricultural work that may be directed as indicated above.

.... Applicant.
Endorsed by .... Parent or Guardian."

The form carried on its opposite side statements showing the character of crop and its value, the amount paid for seeds and an itemized statement of the returns. The school gardens proved an admirable success. The children had learned the details of a great historical event in their own state—the giving out of free land; the boys had conducted a miniature survey; rivalry had been developed in the competition over plots; the gardens, laid out side by side, served as a splendid object lesson in quality of work; no boy or girl could allege a teacher's unfairness from an untilled, weedy plot; the parents were made to feel that the school was doing something practical for their children; the children were taught a simple form of accounting and cost-keeping; and, best of all, they were made to feel their citizenship in the school.

The Department of Agriculture has, in addition to its experimental farm, a well-equipped laboratory, in which tests and experiments are carried on. Sleepy Eye is located in a dairy section; therefore one of the chief functions of this laboratory has been the testing of milk. Any farmer may bring milk samples and have the Babcock test applied to determine the percentage of butter fat which an individual cow is yielding.

IV A Short Course for Busy People

In the neighborhood of Sleepy Eye, as in many other places, there are many boys and girls who cannot attend school throughout the year, but who would welcome a chance to go to school in the winter months. Agricultural colleges have recognized this need by the organization of "short courses" during the winter months. Only a few children can go to college, however. Lack of preparation and lack of funds compel them to remain at home. It was for them that the school at Sleepy Eye organized a short course like that given in the agricultural colleges, extending from the end of November to the middle of March. Of the pupils attending this course, some of the boys are as old as thirty-seven, and some of the girls as young as fifteen; yet all come, eager to find out some of the things which the school has to teach them.

The agricultural work of the short course centered around the agricultural problems of the Brown County Farm. Planting, milk and cream testing, work in seed testing and germination, and treatment of seeds for fungus growths, corn judging, and similar topics covered the work of the term. The short course boys had already learned many lessons in the practical school of farm work. The school at Sleepy Eye offered them in addition the knowledge which science has recently accumulated regarding the work of the farm.

As the successful farmer must be a trained mechanic, the short course laid great stress on manual training. The boys were taught how to handle and care for tools, how to frame a building, how to make eveners, hayracks, watering troughs, wagon boxes, and similar useful farm articles. In the blacksmith shop the simpler problems in forging were covered, including the making of hooks, clevises, cold chisels and other small tools.

While the boys were engaged in agricultural and mechanical work the girls took domestic science. In addition to the elementary work in cooking and sewing there were advanced courses in dress designing, so planned as to prepare a girl to work out her own patterns and make up her own materials.

Let no one suppose that the short course neglected academic work. Indeed, it was originally intended to enable boys and girls who felt too big for the local school, or who had no time to take the entire term there, to review common school subjects. The courses in industrial work, in agriculture and in domestic science were offered in addition to these regular school studies.

The proof of the pudding is in the eating. The boys and girls who take the short course for the first year come back in considerable numbers to take a second and a third year of work during the winter months. The short course is a success, because it gives the boys and girls who take it training and knowledge which they would not otherwise acquire.

V Letting the Boys Do It

The school at Sleepy Eye needed a farm building on the school farm. The short course boys and some of the older boys in the school were anxious to learn. What more natural procedure than for the school to buy the lumber and have the boys do the work? Exactly this proceeding was followed, and the pupils erected the building which they needed to carry on the applied work of the school.

The mechanical work of the school is splendidly organized. First of all, the pupils built a large part of the equipment themselves. Five simple forges, made by the students of pineboards and concrete, form an excellent shop equipment, besides giving the boys who did the work an inkling of the ease with which a forge can be erected in connection with the tool-house on the farm. The boys built a turning lathe, on which the wood turning of the school is done. Besides the shop-work there is a well-organized course in mechanical drawing. The whole department is prepared to teach boys, particularly farm boys, some of the things which they will most need in the mechanical work on the farms.

The mechanical courses are open to the boys in the grades, as well as to the high school and the short course pupils. The work is graded, and may be followed through the high school course.

VI A Look at the Domestic Science

While the boys are in the shops the girls are occupied with domestic science. A well-equipped laboratory and sewing-room furnish the basis for some thorough work. The Domestic Science Department is one to which Mr. Cederstrom points with justifiable pride. "Of all my constructive work since coming here," he says, "I probably take my greatest pride in our Domestic Science Department, where elementary and advanced work is offered in cooking and in household economy."

Because the space in the school was small, and the demand for instruction large, Mr. Cederstrom planned the domestic science tables himself, and superintended their building. Again the effectiveness of the school's work is shown by its results. With the modest equipment which the funds and space available provided, the girls in the Domestic Science Department each year serve a dinner to the farmers and farmers' wives attending the annual farmers' institute held in the school in February. On one occasion the department baked almost half a cord of bread, roasted one hundred and forty pounds of beef, and fed five hundred and seventeen persons at one dinner.

The sewing work includes a complete course in dressmaking. Students are required to make patterns from pictures selected in fashion magazines. These patterns are then used in cutting out the garments, which the girls themselves make up.

Each girl in the High School is required to take at least one year each of cooking and of sewing. These courses occupy five periods a week. An additional year in each course is optional. Most of the girls eagerly elect it. Mr. Cederstrom takes a very practical view of such educational matters. "Our girls like the domestic science work," he says. "They take as much pride in bringing to my office a good loaf of bread, or a well-prepared dish of vegetables or meat as they do in being able to give a perfect demonstration of a theorem in geometry, or a perfect conjugation or declension of a Latin word. Possibly ten years from now they may have more demand upon their ability to prepare a square meal for a hungry life companion, or to cut out a dress or apron for a younger member of the family than they will have need of doing some of the other things which I have just mentioned."

They do not teach domestic science for its own sake out in Sleepy Eye; they see farther ahead than that. Mr. Cederstrom is making his work practical, because, as he says, "We are anxious to do what little we can toward making our girls more efficient and capable as housekeepers, wives, and possibly as mothers."

VII How It Works Out

There are two questions that naturally arise: First, what is the effect of this work on the children? Second, what is its effect on the farmers? Both questions must be answered briefly, though the answers to both might be followed out through pages of illustrative detail.

The children like the school at Sleepy Eye. The boys and girls come early and stay late. The school doors open at eight o'clock and are not closed until dark. There are always pupils there from the beginning to the end of that period. The children are not interested in the applied work alone. Their interest in that has led them very often to an interest in some of the academic studies toward which they had no particular inclination.

The homes in Sleepy Eye are also interested in the school. As one woman remarked: "My girls like to do work about the house now; they never did before." School work which gives girls a new desire and a new viewpoint on the work in the home is a step, and a long one, toward building sounder homes and stronger family ties. There are some Sleepy Eye homes in which the interest of the boys in the school shops has led their parents to buy benches and tools which the children may use at home.

The school at Sleepy Eye has interested the farmers. It has persuaded them that high grade seed is better than mongrel seed. Consequently the farmers are shelling more bushels of corn to the acre planted. The school has persuaded the farmers that well-bred cattle are more profitable than mongrel cattle. Consequently the farmers are raising the standard of their herds. When the farmers come into Sleepy Eye they go to the school. Perhaps they have milk to be tested; perhaps they are looking for suggestions regarding soil or blight; perhaps they want to know the latest facts about the scale or rust; perhaps they want some advice about farm implements. In any case they go to the school.

The farmers have been led to the school through the children. The boys have gone home to their fathers with suggestions and improvements of inestimable value in the management of the farm. The girls have gone home to their mothers with practical ideas on the running of the household. These demonstrations of school efficiency have done more than argument or persuasion ever could hope to do in convincing the fathers and mothers of the usefulness of the school.

VIII Theoretical and Practical

The work in mechanics seems to interfere in no essential particular with the regular academic work of the school. The boys and girls are interested and enthusiastic. That counts for a great deal. Then, too, boys and girls come to school for the mechanical work who would not come at all if the mechanical work were not there. The academic work which such boys take is clear gain. Through the mechanical work many pupils become interested in the school, and the school means, for all pupils, academic as well as applied work.

"We do not discount those parts of an education that were once the sum total of the work in every high school," Mr. Cederstrom says. "They are all offered and taken by the students. We are trying to give in addition to these academic branches the kind of education which will appeal to the children as being of a common-sense order." There is in the high school a Latin Course, a Scientific Course, beside the Agricultural Course and the Industrial Course. All of the students are required to take this academic work. Many, in addition, take the industrial and agricultural work, even when they do not receive credit in their academic course. Each high school student is allowed two periods a day in laboratory work, shop-work, or some other form of applied education. In addition to those periods, the students may work in the shops or laboratory after school, if they please. Many of them get their applied education in that way.

How great is the fire that a little spark kindles! It was more than a thousand miles away that I first heard of the school at Sleepy Eye. It happened in this way. The clock had scarcely announced that it was high noon when a group of men drew their chairs up to a dinner table generously loaded with country hotel fare. There were two school directors in this happen-so party, a carter, a salesman, a lawyer, a farmer and two teachers, who talked with a professional twang. The salesman listened impatiently to the educational clap-trap, watching for an opening between phrases. When at last the loophole appeared:

"Gentlemen," said he, "you're interested in schools? Then you ought to see some real schools. Did you ever go to a school to listen to a phonograph?" Then, turning to the farmers: "Did you ever go to school to get your horses shod? You go to school for both in Sleepy Eye, Minnesota. They're the greatest schools I have ever seen. They run from seven in the morning till eight at night, and accommodate every kid that wants an education. Gentlemen, if you want to see real schools go to Sleepy Eye."

CHAPTER XII

THE SOUTH FOR THE NEW EDUCATION

I A Dream of Empire

A keen Atlanta business man leaned forward on his chair and spoke eagerly. "Yes, sir," he exclaimed, "the world is ours. We have the biggest, finest batch of undeveloped resources in the country—perhaps on the planet. Iron, coal, stone, timber, power—our hills are full of them, so full that we have never even inventoried our treasure-house. Our possibilities are beyond the power of words, and we've got to live up to them."

This man knew Georgia and the South. He had helped, and still is helping to convert the iron, coal, timber, and water-power into Southern prosperity. He was still unsatisfied.

"The trouble with us is, we can't go fast enough," he admitted. "Do you know why? Do you know the biggest burden we have to carry—the most determined enemy we have to fight? Well, sir, it's ignorance—the ignorance of the common man about his farm or his trade; the ignorance of the business man about outside things; the ignorance of the teachers who are supposed to enlighten us." He leaned forward again. "That sounds strong, doesn't it? But it's gospel."

I reminded him of the rapidity with which the South was forging ahead in its educational activities. He threw his head back proudly. "Of course," he cried, "the experiment stations, the colleges, the high schools, the club movement, and all that—of course we're going ahead. I'm not speaking of that. My point is that we must wake up to two things. First of all, we must never make the mistakes that you did in the North when you built up your educational system. That means no pedantry, or classical snobbery. We mustn't go that way. Our way is plain though. I see it more clearly every time I think the matter over—we must train the intelligence of the Southern people."

He continued, in his enthusiastic mood. "Yes, there is a great future for the South. Its resources make a future possible; but unless those resources are intelligently used, our prosperity will not go very deep, or reach very far. We must take the people with us."

This man's view typifies the educational vision that is sweeping over the South. "We must take the people with us," he said. There is nothing novel in the idea; but coming as it did from a representative business man, it carried weight and conviction.

Another thing he said in the same connection enforced his argument. "They talk about the race problem in the South," he said. "That is, the old generation does. We younger men are not so much concerned about the race problem as we are concerned about efficiency in industry and in agriculture. The races are here to stay; we cannot change that if we would. Meanwhile, all of us, whites as well as blacks, are slovenly in our farming, indifferent in our business transactions, and hopelessly behind in our methods of conducting affairs. From top to bottom we need trained intelligence. That, more than anything else, will solve the South's problems."

II Finding the Way

The step is a short one from a vision of trained intelligence to a demand for effective education. Throughout the South, the will to progress is everywhere in evidence, and with unerring accuracy, one community after another is turning to this as the way.

There is no Southern city in which the agitation for increased educational activity is not being pushed with vigor and intensity. On all hands there appears the result of a conviction that the only means by which the effectiveness of the South can be maintained and increased, lie along the path of increased educational opportunities. The South, if it is to fulfill the greatness of its promise, must remodel its educational system in the interests of a larger South, as the West has remodeled its educational system in the interest of a larger West. The notable State universities of the Middle and Far West, the Normal Schools, the prevalent system of education, have been felt, and are now being felt, in the progressive, efficient, Western population. Nothing less than a generally educated public could have made the West in the brief years that have elapsed since it was a wilderness. Nothing save general education can make the resources of the South yield up their greatest advantage to the Southern people.

The time for traditional formalism has passed in the South, as it has passed in every other progressive community. Whatever the needs of the community may be, those needs must be met through some form of public education. In the South the most pressing need appears in the demand for intelligent farming. For decades the tenant farmers, largely negroes, cultivated their farms as their fathers had cultivated. They raised cotton because the raising of cotton offered the path of least resistance. Farm animals were scarce, because the farm animals only came with surplus cash, and surplus cash was scarce indeed in districts where the tenant farmers lived through the year on the credit obtained from the prospective cotton crops. There was little corn raised, because the people did not understand the need for raising corn, nor did they realize the financial possibilities of the Southern corn crop. In a word, the agricultural South lacked the knowledge which modern scientific agriculture has brought.

The past generation has seen a revolution in Southern agriculture, because of the revolution which has occurred in Southern agricultural education. Led by the experiment stations and universities, the South has undertaken to reorganize its system of living from the land.

The Atlanta banker fully realized the need for culture. He was himself a cultured gentleman; but he also saw that before the people of the South could have culture, they must have an economic system directed with sufficient intelligence to supply the necessaries of life, which must always be taken for granted before the possibilities of culture are realized. Cultural education comes after, and not before, education for intelligent and direct vocational activity.

During the educational revolution of the past twenty-five years, no section of the country has thrown itself into the foreground of educational progress with more vigor and with greater earnestness and zeal than that displayed in the South. In certain directions the South has proved a leader in the inauguration and administration of new activities. In other directions the Southern States have followed actively and energetically.

A traveler through the New South stumbles unavoidably upon countless illustrations of the part which modern education is playing in Southern life. Individuals, families, communities, are being re-made by the new education.

III Jem's Father

Jem wasn't a good boy, but he was interested in his school. He was one of those fortunate boys who lived in a county that had been possessed by the corn club idea, and the corn club was the thing which had given Jem his school interest.

Jem never took to studies. Each year he had told his mother that "there weren't no use in goin' back to that there school again." Persistently she had sent him back, until one year when Jem found a reason for going.

A new teacher came to Jem's school—a young man fresh from normal school, full of enthusiasm, energy, and new ideas. The boys felt from the start that he was their friend, and before many weeks had elapsed, the community began to feel his presence. This new teacher was particularly enthusiastic over the "club idea." "We must get the boys and girls doing something together" he kept saying to his classes.

The year wore on, but interest in the school did not flag, because all through the winter months there were entertainments, parents' meetings, literary meetings, spelling bees, reading hours, and other evening activities. In fact, the time came when there was a light in the school-house three or four nights in each week.

Toward spring the new teacher began to push the "club idea." He started with the boys, and, as luck would have it, picked out Jem. "Jem," he said one day, "I want you to stay after school, I want to speak to you a minute." Jem stayed, not knowing exactly what was coming. When the rest of the pupils had tumbled out of the school door, and disappeared along the muddy road, the teacher and Jem sat down together.

"Jem," said the teacher, "we ought to have a corn club in this school."

Jem looked up doggedly, but gave no sign of interest or enthusiasm.

"You see," the teacher said, "it's this way. Farming isn't all that it might be around here. People raise things the way they have always been raised. Our county superintendent has an idea. He proposes to teach the farmers in this county how to raise corn."

Jem looked skeptical. "Are you to do the teaching?" he asked.

"No," was the answer, "you are."

"I?" said Jem.

"Yes," said the teacher, "you and the other boys in the school."

Jem scratched his head. "I ain't never taught no one nothing in my life," he commented.

"It's this way," the teacher went on. "Up at Washington and out at the State College they have been doing a lot of thinking and working with corn. They found, for instance, that if you pick seed corn carefully, you get a better crop than if you are careless in seed selection. They have also found that if you follow certain rules about planting and cultivation you get a better crop. For years the men at the Experiment Station and at Washington talked about these things in Farmers' Bulletins. They established experiment farms, and demonstration farms, too. Lately they have been doing something more, and something which I think is better than anything so far—they have decided to have the boys teach their fathers how to raise corn."

"Do you mean to say," asked Jem, "that I could teach Dad anything about corn-raisin'?"

"Yes," said the teacher, "you can, and, what is more, you will, won't you?"

"Well," said Jem, "I dunno."

"Here is what we have to do," said the teacher. "This year the county superintendent is going to offer prizes for the boy with the best acre of corn. He sends out rules. You have to plough a certain way, plant a certain way, and cultivate a certain way. If you do not follow the rules you are not allowed to stay in the contest. Now I'll tell you what I want to do. The boys in this school are as smart, if not smarter, than the boys in any other school in the country; so I guess it is up to us to get some of those prizes right here at home."

Jem was visibly interested. "Money prizes?" he asked.

"Yes, money prizes," said the teacher. "The first prize will be fifty dollars."

Jem's eyes opened wide. "I'm in for that," he said with conviction.

That night, when Jem sat down to supper, he broached the corn proposition to his father.

"Shucks," his father exclaimed. "You raise an acre of corn? Why you wouldn't get twenty-five bushels!"

"Twenty-five," said Jem, contemptuously. "I'd get a hundred."

"A hundred," said his father. "Here, look here, boy, I have been farming this land for thirty odd years, and the best I ever done on an acre of corn was seventy bushels. I'll tell you what, though," he added conclusively, "this here talk about corn clubs makes me tired. You and your hundred bushels! I was looking over the paper when it came in this noon, and I saw a piece about a chap over by Southport with over a hundred bushels to the acre. Do you know what I'm goin' to do tonight? I'm goin' to write that editor a letter, and tell him that any paper that publishes lies like that ain't fit for my family to see. This year's subscription ain't run out, but they don't need to send me the rest. I'll get a paper somewhere else."

Despite home opposition, Jem persisted and prevailed. His father gave him an acre grudgingly, but it was a good acre. And when, following the rules which he and the other boys who had agreed to enter the contest read over with the teacher, he disked his land and ploughed his narrow, deep furrows, he listened, not without misgivings, to the remarks which his elder brother passed at his expense.

"Say, Jem," this brother remarked, "you have spent three times as much time on that acre as any acre of corn raised in this county was ever worth. Are you diggin' graves for 'possums?"

When, later in the season, Jem cultivated with persistent regularity, he was forced to listen to similar comments. Jem wasn't good at repartee; so he said nothing; but, sustained by the encouragement of the new teacher, who came to see his acre every week, Jem followed the rules to the letter.

He had his reward at harvest time. When the ears first set it became apparent that Jem had a good crop. As they developed, the goodness of the crop became more manifest; but when the acre had been harvested, put through the sheller and bagged, and Jem had stowed in his pocket a certificate of "ninety-six bushels on one acre," it was time for some explanations.

"Jem," said his father at the supper table on the evening of that memorable day when Jem's corn went through the sheller, and his certificate showed ninety-six bushels, "I wrote a letter to that editor, and sent him next year's subscription in advance."

IV Club Life Militant

The experience of Jem's father has been duplicated many times by parents and communities during the past ten years of club growth in the South. The school, working through the children, has educated fathers, mothers, villages, and whole counties.

All of the agencies of government,—local, State, and national,—have cooperated to make the children's clubs one of the leading agencies in developing that trained intelligence which is so great an asset in the prosperity of any community. Thanks to the tireless efforts of men like William H. Smith, the children's clubs have become one of the most aggressive factors in educating rural communities to higher standards of efficiency. There are many kinds of clubs—corn clubs, potato clubs, tomato clubs, pig clubs. Anything which the children can raise is a legitimate object of club activity. The work in the South started with corn clubs.

The corn-club idea in Mississippi grew out of an educational experience of Professor William H. Smith.[24] For years Professor Smith had taught, in a mildly progressive way, the time-honored subjects which were included in the study-course of the rural school. Two of Professor Smith's students, a boy of twenty and a girl of seventeen, left school; and they left, as the boy told Professor Smith very frankly, because the school taught them very little that would be of use later on in the work which they would be called upon to do. This boy expected to grow cotton; the girl expected to marry the boy, manage his domestic affairs and attend to the many duties which fall to the lot of women on a farm.

When he left school, the boy put it to Professor Smith in this way: "I am goin' to be a farmer. I ain't fitted to be nothing else, and book learnin' ain't helpin' me none. It's just a waste of time. I've got to clear land and work it into a farm. If I was goin' to be a bookkeeper or an engineer, or somethin', what you are teachin' me here might help; but I can't remember that I have ever learned a thing since I got the hang how to figure the interest on a mortgage, that will be of any account to me on a farm. Almost all the boys has got to be a farmer like me. You know, professor, it appears to me like these schools for the people ought to be teachin' the children of the people how to make a livin' on the farm—how to make life better and easier, instead of just makin' us plum disgusted with ourselves."

This experience, standing out among a multitude of similar experiences, led Professor Smith to an interest in some form of educational work that would help boys and girls in their lives on the farm. The outcome of his thinking and experimenting, combined with the thinking and experimenting of many another capable educational leader, is the club idea for boys and girls alike.

There was a real need for the corn club. For the year 1899 the total corn area in Alabama was 2,743,060 acres. On these acres the farmers secured an average of 12.7 bushels per acre. Ten years later, in 1909, the total acreage had decreased to 2,572,092, and the per acre yield had decreased to 11.9 bushels per acre. Here was a decrease of 170,968 acres in corn; of 4,367,310 bushels in the corn crop; and of .8 of a bushel in the average yield per acre. The boys' corn club movement was started in Alabama in 1909. That year two hundred and sixty-five boys were enrolled. The average per acre yield of corn in the State was 11.9 bushels. The next year the enrollment of boys reached twenty-one hundred; the total yield increased more than sixty per cent.; and the average number of bushels per acre rose to eighteen. The figures for 1911 and 1912 show an increase, though less extensive, in the total acreage and the total yield of corn for each year.

Southern land will grow corn. Properly treated, it will better a yield of twelve bushels per acre, five, ten, and even fifteen-fold. The leaders of Southern agricultural education knew this. They knew, furthermore, that the betterment could never be brought about until the farmers were convinced that it was possible. How could they be shown? The Farmers' Bulletin had a place; the experiment farm had a place; but if it were only possible to make every farm an experiment farm!

The way lay through the boys. They could be induced to organize miniature experiments in scores of farms in every county, and then the farmers would see!

Backed by a carefully worked out organization, the authorities set out with the deliberate purpose of educating the farmer through his son. If his corn yield was low, he would learn how to get a larger yield. If he raised no corn, he would learn of the spot-cash value of corn. Boys were organized into clubs; directions were given; prizes were offered, and the boys went to work with a will. For the most part they took one acre.

When compared to the yield on surrounding acres, the corn crops secured by the boys are little short of phenomenal. In Pike County, Alabama, where the number of boys engaging in corn club contests increased from one in 1910 to two hundred and seventy in 1912, the average number of bushels per acre grown by the boys rose from 50.5 to 85.3. In the entire State there were one hundred and thirty-seven boys who made over a hundred bushels per acre each in 1911. The average per acre for each of these boys was one hundred and twenty-seven bushels, and the total profit on their corn crop was $12,500.

Records made by individual boys through the Southern States run very high. Claude McDonald, of Hamer, S. C., raised $210^{4}/_{7}$ bushels at a cost of 33.3¢ a bushel. Junius Hill, of Attalla, Ala., raised $212^{1}/_{2}$ bushels. Ben Leath, of Kensington, Ga., raised $214^{5}/_{7}$ bushels. John Bowen, of Grenada, Miss., raised $221^{1}/_{5}$ bushels. Eber A. Kimbrough, Alexander City, Ala., raised $224^{3}/_{4}$ bushels; and Bebbie Beeson, Monticello, Miss., raised $227^{1}/_{16}$ bushels.[25] These boys were all State prize winners.

There are several things worthy of note about these record yields. Practically all of the high yields were made on deeply ploughed, widely separated rows. The record made by Bennie Beeson ($227^1/_{16}$ bushels, at a cost of fourteen cents per bushel) was secured on dark, upland soil, with a clay sub-soil, ploughing to a depth of ten inches, rows three feet apart, hills six inches apart, with ten cultivations. Beeson used $5^1/_2$ tons of manure and eight dollars' worth of other fertilizer on his acre. The seed corn was New Era. Barnie Thomas, who grew 225 bushels on rich, sandy loam, ploughed nine inches, planted his rows three and one-half feet apart, and kept the hills ten inches apart. He cultivated six times, and selected his own seed from the field. Many of the boys making the fine records developed and selected their own seed. One boy, with an acre yield of 124.9 bushels, cleared six hundred and ninety-five dollars, counting prizes. Another boy, with a yield of $97^4/_5$ bushels, reports that his father's yield was thirty bushels. John Bowen, with a yield of $221^1/_5$ bushels, reports the yield on nearby acres as forty bushels. Arthur Hill, with $180^3/_5$ bushels, reports the nearby yields as twenty bushels.

Such figures, uncertified, would challenge the credulity of the uninitiated. The land on which these record yields were secured had been raising twenty, forty, and fifty bushels of corn to the acre. Over great sections, the per acre average was well under twenty. Into this desolation of agricultural inefficiency, a few thousand school boys entered. Under careful supervision and proper guidance, with little additional expenditure of money or of time, they produced results wholly unbelievable to the old-time farmer. Yet he saw the crop, husked, and watched it through the sheller. There was no magic and no chicanery. He had learned a lesson.

The records cited above are exceptionally high. There were hundreds of others almost equally good. "Twenty-one Georgia club members from the seventh congressional district alone grew 2,641 bushels at an average cost of 23 cents per bushel; 19 boys in Gordon County, Georgia, average 90 bushels, 10 of them making 1,058 bushels. The 10 boys who stood highest in Georgia averaged 169.9 bushels and made a net profit of more than $100 each, besides prizes won. In Alabama 100 boys average 97 bushels at an average cost of 27 cents. In Monroe County, Alabama, 25 boys averaged 78 bushels. In Yazoo County, Mississippi, 21 boys averaged 111.6 bushels at an average cost of 19.7 cents. In Lee County, Mississippi, 17 boys averaged 82 bushels at an average cost of 21 cents. Sixty-five boys in Mississippi averaged 109.9 bushels at an average cost of 25 cents. Twenty Mississippi boys averaged 140.6 bushels at an average cost of 23 cents. Ninety-two boys in Louisiana grew 5,791 bushels on 92 acres; 10 of these boys had above 100 bushels each, although the weather conditions were very unfavorable in that State. In North Carolina 100 boys averaged 99 bushels. In the same State 432 boys averaged 63 bushels. In Buncombe County, North Carolina, 10 boys averaged 88 bushels. In Sussex County, Virginia, 16 boys averaged 82 bushels. Fifteen boys in the vicinity of Memphis, Tenn., where the business men contributed about $3,000 to aid the work, averaged 127.4 bushels at an average cost of 28 cents per bushel. Many other records in other States were equally good in view of the fact that a drought prevailed very generally throughout the South in 1911.["][26]

Such returns challenge the attention of the most hidebound. These boys got results that exceeded anything that had ever been heard of in their communities. The old folks who had scoffed; the wise-acres whose advice was not taken; and the "I told you so" farmers who had uttered their predictions, all stood aside, while the boys, pointer in hand, taught their respective communities one of the best lessons they had ever learned.

V Canning Clubs

Parallel with the boys' corn clubs are the girls' canning clubs. If the boys could grow corn (in a number of cases the corn contests were won by girls), why might it not be possible to have the girls do something along parallel lines? The idea found expression in the girls' tomato clubs and similar organizations. During 1910, three hundred and twenty-five girls were enrolled in such clubs in Virginia and South Carolina. Dr. Knapp and his fellow workers decided that one-tenth of an acre would be enough for a good garden. Each girl was urged to plant some other kind of vegetable in addition to her tomatoes, and to can surplus fruit. In 1911, more than three thousand girls, in eight different States, had joined clubs and planted their gardens. By 1912 the number had grown to twenty-three thousand girls in twelve States. Many of the girls put up more than five hundred quart cans of tomatoes from their plots, besides ketchup, pickles, chow-chow, preserves, and other products. Quite a number of girls put up more than a thousand quart cans, and one girl put up fifteen hundred quart cans. Some of the girls, in addition to the prizes, had a net profit of as much as a hundred dollars on their gardens.

The United States Bureau of Plant Industry sets forth the object of the girls' demonstration work as follows:

> "(1) To encourage rural families to provide purer and better food at a lower cost, and utilize the surplus and otherwise waste products of the orchard and garden, and make the poultry yard an effective part of the farm economy.
>
> (2) To stimulate interest and wholesome cooperation among members of the family in the home.
>
> (3) To provide some means by which girls may earn money at home, and, at the same time, get the education and viewpoint necessary for the ideal farm life.
>
> (4) To open the way for practical demonstrations in home economics.
>
> (5) To furnish earnest teachers a plan for aiding their pupils and helping their communities."[27]

VI Recognition Day for Boys and Girls

The most astonishing thing about the club activity is the recognition which it has won wherever it has been worked out on an extensive basis. The reason for this general recognition is quite obvious, and its effect is no less stimulating.

Public officials and business men have vied with one another in their efforts to reward the winners of county and State club contests. The same bulletin which records the astonishing figures on corn yields, tells about the things that were done for the 56,840 boys who were members of corn clubs. Fifty-two Georgia boys received diplomas signed by the governor of the State and other officials, for producing more than a hundred bushels per acre each, at an average cost of less than thirty cents per bushel. Business men and citizens generally subscribed liberally money, free railroad transportation, and trips to State capitals. In 1911 the total value of the prizes offered in the South to the boys' corn clubs approximated fifty thousand dollars. In Oklahoma, one thousand dollars in gold was offered to the one hundred and twenty boys making the best record in that State. The State prize winners were sent to Washington for a week, where they were received at the White House by the President, and at the Capitol by the Speaker of the House of Representatives. They were presented with special cards of admission to the Senate and House of Representatives, and, when visiting Congress, they were presented to their Senators and Congressmen. By special invitation these distinguished visitors appeared before the Committee on Agriculture at the House of Representatives. They also visited the office of the Secretary of Agriculture. They were photographed, and large diplomas bearing the seal of the Department and the signature of the Secretary were awarded to them.

One does not wonder at the widespread recognition accorded these boys, in view of the fact that their efforts have been responsible for an immense increase in the business prosperity of their respective States. Once more have educators demonstrated the possibilities of teaching parents through the education of children.

VII Teaching Grown-Ups to Read

The educational work which is being done in the uplands of the South has already received widespread recognition. The slogan, "Down with the moonshine still and up with the moonlight school," typifies the spirit of the upland community.

One might journey far before discovering a more enthusiastic people than the teachers and the scholars of the Southern uplands. The appalling extent of illiteracy among the descendants of Marion's men finds a parallel in their pathetic desire for some form of education.

The Southern hill whites love the old and fear the new. Traditionally, they belong to a past generation; actually, they are reaching out for the better things which the new generation can offer. The moonlight schools are attended by old people and young alike. The struggling colleges, the industrial and technical schools, with their record of privation and hardship, bear eloquent testimony to the genuine efforts which the upland population is making in these early years of its educational awakening.

Every sincere effort among the hill whites meets with instant response. For the most part, they deprive themselves of the necessaries of life in order that they may send their children to school. Boys skimp and save; girls walk for miles along mountain trails and paths; communities give of the scanty means of their effort for the building and maintenance of schools. Everywhere the spirit of the new education is permeating the Southern upland communities.

VIII George Washington, Junior

One teacher, whose years of effort in the Piedmont have brought her the confidence and co-operation of the community, tells of the success of one of her earliest ventures with a boy of thirteen.

The boy's father was bad; his mother slovenly and indifferent. The boy himself was bright and active.

When the time came for him to enter the cotton mill, the teacher protested to his family, but without success. Still there was something that she could do for him, still she saw an opportunity of serving him, and she asked him to come to her home with a number of other boys, for a couple of nights a week, when they sat together, reading, or playing games.

The boy had appeared sullen at first, but toward the end of his school term he showed an active interest. It became apparent that he was particularly clever at languages. None of his lessons troubled him, and, with the assistance of the teacher, he learned Italian readily, and during the evenings, when the other boys played games or talked, he worked over his Italian sentences with vital interest.

Just before Christmas, during the first year that this boy had spent in the mill, a friend visited his teacher, became interested in her work, and asked if there was any way in which she could help.

"You may," said the teacher. "You may buy Andy an outfit."

The friend went to the city with the order in her pocket,—a hat, a suit, and a complete outfit, new, as a Christmas present for Andy.

On Christmas eve, Andy alone came to the teacher's house. She had not asked the other boys,—partly because most of them preferred to stay at home, partly because she had no such fine present for them as she had for Andy.

"Never in my life," the teacher said, "had I seen Andy clean. I made up my mind that for once he should have a clean body as well as clean clothes."

When Andy came that Christmas eve, the teacher took him into a room where there were towels, soap, a basin, and a new outfit of clothes.

"Andy," she said, "this is your Christmas present from my friend, and now you are going to give me a Christmas present, too. You are going to wash up and dress up."

Andy followed directions, and when he emerged from the room in his spick and span outfit, his hat set side-wise on his wet, newly combed hair, he stood up very straight, surveying himself as best he could from head to foot, and exclaimed,—"Gee! I feel just like George Washington." The bath and the new suit were a realization of his highest ideal.

"Andy and I were always friends after that," said the teacher, "and since Andy was the moving spirit among the boys in the village, the boys and I got along well together. It was my introduction to the heart of the community, and it came with Andy's realization of an ideal which he had long cherished."

IX A Step Toward Good Health

Having won Andy over, the teacher prepared to work her way past some of the barriers of prejudice which the community had placed between itself and civilization. The girls offered the readiest opening.

"The homes were wretched," the teacher said. "The people did not know the simplest health rules. They were strangers to sanitation or cleanliness.

Their housekeeping was primitive and their cooking miserable. I had won the boys by getting them together in something that resembled a club. I decided that my best path to the girls, and from them to the community, lay through housekeeping."

The hypothesis was, at least, worthy of a try-out. The teacher began by keeping her own house in the most approved manner, and asking the girls to come in and help her do it.

"You'll like to take supper with me this evening," she would say to a group of girls at recess time. "Speak to your mothers when you go home, and you, Sadie and Annie, will stay over night and sleep in the spare bed."

They were slow to respond at first. Long habit made them suspicious, but when the first few girls had spent their night with the teacher and had come home with the tales of her wonderful household arrangements, the others were looking eagerly for a chance to duplicate their experiences.

"Am I next?" a little girl asked anxiously one day, after the invitations to a party had been given out. The assurance that she was, made her face shine for the remainder of the afternoon.

"The school girls all came willingly," the teacher said. "It was after I had them so interested that one of the factory hands came in. It was Saturday night, and she rapped on the door before coming in with a hesitating touch, as if she was afraid. She sat down across from me, smoothing her dress and looking unhappy."

"You'll not understand," said the factory girl, apologetically. "But Mame is in your school—she's my sister. You had her up last week to spend the night. You'll remember?"

The teacher nodded.

"She came home, and ever since she's been telling us about the way you did things. And I've been thinking,——"

She stopped and looked at the teacher, half suspiciously, half appealingly.

"I've been thinking how nice it would be for me, if I could do them things the same as you. You see," she spoke rapidly, "I'm gettin' married soon now, and when Mame came a-telling that way, and our house like it always is, and the baby crying, and nothing done exceptin' ma a-scoldin', and I says to myself, I says, if I could do things like that teacher can do 'em mebbe I wouldn't make mistakes like ma makes 'em." She paused for breath, looking expectant.

"You would like to come here to see how I do things?" the teacher asked.

The girl nodded eagerly.

"Come Monday after hours, and spend the night with me."

"After that," the teacher said, "it was a great deal easier. The next thing I wanted to do was to get the children examined for glasses and throat trouble. There were two second-rate country doctors there who knew little or nothing about modern medicine. The nearest man that I could trust was forty miles away. He was a specialist, too, and high priced. Still, I sat down and wrote him a letter, telling him how we were fixed. He answered by return mail, making a special rate and setting a day. I hoped to take twelve of the children, but I had car fare for only seven. Then came our windfall. I told the railroad what I was trying to do, and they made a special excursion rate and took the children at less than half fare. We were all able to go, and the extra money went for a treat to soda and the movies."

The children went back home, singing the praises of the trip, the teacher, and the doctor. They went back, too, with expert advice and assistance, and with the good news that others would soon have a turn.

Group by group, the needy children were brought down to the specialist in the city. Some were even operated on, although at the outset the parents would not hear of operations. In the end the children won, however. Their enthusiasm for the teacher and their doctor carried the day.

"It has been slow," the teacher said, "but at the end of it all, they see better, hear better, eat more wholesome, nourishing food, live better, and understand themselves better. On the whole it has paid."

X Theory and Practice[28]

The rural schools of the South have no monopoly on progressive educational views. A number of Southern cities have taken up their position in the vanguard of educational progress. Notable among these cities is Columbus, Georgia,—a city of 20,554 people, in which Superintendent Roland B. Daniel has undertaken a vigorous policy of shaping the schools in the interests of the community. There were in 1913, 5,356 children of school age in Columbus. Of this number, 4,089 were in the schools. The school population is rather unevenly divided, racially,—3,348 of the children of school age are white, and 1,198 are colored. About one-quarter of the white population depends for its livelihood upon the mills. Columbus is surrounded by an agricultural district from which come many children in search of high school training. The city of Columbus presents an industrial problem of an unusually complex character, and the manner in which this problem has been handled by the schools is worthy of the highest commendation. Superintendent Daniel has laid down three definite planks in his educational platform for the city of Columbus. In the first place, he aims to provide school accommodations which are fitted to the peculiar needs of each part of the community. In the second place, he aims to shape the school system of Columbus in terms of the local environment of the children. In the third place, he has inaugurated a high school policy, which makes high school training practical as well as theoretical.

Among the mill operatives of Columbus, Superintendent Daniel estimates that there are approximately 800 children of school age. The situation presented by these children was critical in the extreme. There was an absence of compulsory education laws; few of the children attended any school, and when they did enter a school they seldom remained long enough to secure any marked educational advantage. Less than 5 per cent. of the children continued in school after they were old enough to work in the cotton mills.

Pursuant of his intention to make the schools supply the needs of all of the children of Columbus, Superintendent Daniel organized the North Highlands School in the factory district. Of this school he says: "It is not made to conform, either in course of study or hours, to the other schools of similar rank in the system, for the board desires to meet the conditions and convenience of the people for whom the school was established. Classroom work begins in the morning at 8 o'clock and continues until 11 o'clock, with a recess of 10 minutes at 9:30. The afternoon session begins at 1 o'clock, and the school closes for the day at 3:30 o'clock."

The long intermission in the middle of the day is given in order to allow the children to take hot lunches to parents, brothers, and sisters who are working in the mill. Many of the mills are located at some distance from the school. Some of the children are called upon to walk as much as two miles during the noon hour, in order to carry the lunches. These "dinner toters," when carrying lunch baskets for persons outside of the family, receive 25 cents per week per basket. In case several baskets are carried, the income thus earned is considerable.

The school thus organized on the basis of local needs is further specialized in a way that will appeal to the needs of the mill operative group. The academic courses are similar to the courses offered in the other schools, except that more emphasis is laid upon the "three R's." Superintendent Daniel says that the time is very limited in which these children will attend school, and more attention is given as to what may be regarded as fundamental. "While the prescribed course contemplates seven years, few continue after the fifth or sixth year, so strong is the call of the mills. Not more than 1 per cent finish this school and pursue their studies further."

The three morning hours and the first hour in the afternoon are devoted to academic studies, while the last hour and a half of the day is given to practical work. The boys are required to take elementary courses in woodwork and gardening, alternating these two branches on alternate days. The girls are given work in basketry, sewing, cooking, poultry raising, and gardening.

The results of the introduction of this applied work are summed up by Superintendent Daniel in this way,—"In all of these lines of work it is now the hope of the school only to better living conditions a little among the people for whom it was especially organized. The transformation is necessarily slow. In the beginning, no doubt, the advocates of this type of school thought that many might be induced to continue in school and do more advanced work, especially along vocational lines. In this respect the school has been a disappointment to some. We are seldom able to induce pupils to finish even the limited course offered in this school."

The North Highland School, in addition to its work for the children, has begun an organized effort to raise the standards of the local community. Every day the principal and teachers of the school visit some of the homes, giving helpful suggestions, caring for the sick, and in any other possible way contributing to home life. Superintendent Daniel reports the progress in this respect by saying,—"Confidence is now so strong that one of the teachers every Saturday morning collects the physically defective ones in the community and takes them to the free clinic for operations or treatment. At first parents would see their children die rather than permit them to be operated upon, but now they seldom decline to permit them to be taken by a teacher to the free clinic, when in the judgment of the teacher it is necessary."

The school has made an effort to organize the older people of the community. There are entertainments and school gatherings in which parents and children alike participate. As a further help to those parents who are compelled to work in the mills, the school grounds, which are amply provided with a full play equipment, are open to all of the children at all hours of the day and all days of the week. "It is not infrequent," says Superintendent Daniel, "that, when the mother goes to work at 6 in the morning, she sends her children to the school to enjoy the privileges of the grounds until the opening of the school at 8 o'clock."

The work of the negro schools is similarly fitted to the industrial needs of the negro children. Boys and girls alike devote a considerable portion of their time to industrial work. The main purpose of this work for negroes is to prepare them for the line of industrial opportunity open to them. The school reports that it has developed a number of good blacksmiths, carpenters, cooks, seamstresses, and laundresses. Pupils who remain in the schools long enough to complete the course are able to earn, upon leaving school, about twice what they would be able to earn had no such training been provided.

A vigorous attempt has been made to reorganize grade work in the interests of clearness and effectiveness. As Superintendent Daniel puts the matter, —"We undertook to place before the teachers a definite problem, and to put suggestions into tangible form. We stated that all subjects could be taught with the books merely as helps and means to an end, and contend further for the doctrine that a working knowledge of books and subjects is far more desirable than accomplishing the feat of memorizing the printed page." Many teachers will be astonished by the doctrine which Superintendent Daniel evolves from this statement of educational theory. "The teachers were asked to conduct the work in such a manner that it would not be necessary to recite or take written tests with closed books, but that school books be used as tools with which to work, and that the child should use text-books as adults do books of reference, while the teacher guides and directs in the development of thought.["]

This attempt of Superintendent Daniel to proceed with the grammar school work in a more natural way, and to relate all of it more closely to life, met with some interesting results, as may be gathered from the following test questions which were worked out by teachers in pursuance of the instructions to make text-books incidental and thought primary in the school work.

ARITHMETIC, THIRD B

Roy shops for his mother at Kirven's. He buys 2 boxes of hair pins at $.05 each, 6 towels at $.10 each, and 5 handkerchiefs for $.25. What was his bill? If he hands the clerk $1.00, how much change will he receive?

THIRD A

If Isabel's 2 pair of shoes cost $4, how much will shoes for all the girls in the class cost?

GEOGRAPHY THIRD B

Turn to the map on page 65 and find and write the names of seven different shore forms.

ARITHMETIC, FOURTH B

In our room are 46 pupils. The class receives 230 tablets and 138 pencils for the term. How many of each does each child receive?

GEOGRAPHY, FOURTH B

What products may be sent to us from New England? If they were shipped from Portsmouth, N. H., on what bodies of water would they travel?

GEOGRAPHY, FOURTH A

Why does the United States carry on more trade with the British Isles than with Germany? At what seaport would our vessels land in the British Isles? What would they carry and what would they bring back?

GEOGRAPHY, FIFTH A

> What highways of trade will be used for shipping oranges from San Francisco to Columbus, Ga., by way of the Panama Canal? How many miles is this, approximately? (Use rule and map on page 65.)
>
> ### GEOGRAPHY, FIFTH B
>
> What is the chief industry of the people of Columbus, and why? Describe the climate of our city, tell what fruits, vegetables and farm products find a market here. What would a boat coming up the river bring to Columbus? What would it carry back?

Superintendent Daniel's viewpoint is clear and sane. "It is not sufficient," he says, "to maintain courses in domestic science and manual training for the grades, and to teach other subjects as if they belonged to another realm." Consequently he has made every endeavor to bring together the forces of the community and of the school in a sympathetic whole, around which the educational life of the town must center.

The industrial high school is an integral and highly important part of the work in the Columbus schools. Side by side with the academic high school, it affords an opportunity for the children who do not intend to continue their educational work beyond high school grade to get some assistance in the direction of a training for life activity. It was originally intended to duplicate, in a measure, the conditions and hours maintained in the industrial plants of the city. Formerly the school was open for eleven calendar months; at the present time a vacation of six weeks is allowed. The school hours are from 8 o'clock in the morning until 4 o'clock in the afternoon, for five days each week. Pupils who have not maintained the required standard during the week are compelled to attend school on Saturday.

All pupils of the Industrial High School are required to take academic work of high school grade in mathematics, history, English, and science.

The introduction of manual training and domestic science into the grades of all Columbus schools has pointed many children in the direction of the Industrial High School. While it is not the intention of the school authorities to make the work of the Industrial High School final, it is hoped that those children who are enabled to continue with educational work are benefited markedly by this specialized course.

Throughout this deliberate attempt of the Columbus school administration to make the schools fit the needs of the community there is evidence of a scientific spirit which is in the last degree commendable. The community need is first ascertained. The school work is then organized in response to this community need. If, perchance, the first effort meets with little success, additional effort is continued until some measure of success is assured. The school authorities are not afraid to change their opinions or their system. They are not even afraid to fail on a given experiment. The one thing of which they are afraid is failure to provide for the educational needs of the community.

XI A People Coming to Its Own

The first great battle in the educational awakening of the South has been won. The people realize the necessity for an intelligently active population.

The second battle is well under way. The people of the South are shaping the schools to meet the peculiar educational needs which the economic and social problems of the South present.

A rallying-cry is ringing through the Southern States,—"The schools for the people; the people for the schools; and a higher standard of education and of life for the community."

The South is in line for the New Education. School officials are working. Superintendent Daniel writes,—"Everyone connected with the system has been too intent on doing his work well and in establishing and maintaining the ideals of the system to be disturbed by petty difficulties. The teachers," he adds, "have appeared to feel that it was rather a privilege than a burden to participate in making the Columbus system efficient through the preparation of her children for life."[29] The public is asking for a correlation of school with life, and the schools are educating the South through the children.

FOOTNOTES:

[24] Now State Superintendent. See an article "'Corn-Club' Smith," P. C. Macfarlane, Collier's Weekly, May 17, 1913, p. 19.

[25] United States Department of Agriculture, Bureau of Plant Industry, Results of Boys' Demonstration Work in Corn Clubs in 1911, Washington, May, 1912, p. 4.

[26] Op. cit., pp. 5-6.

[27] U. S. Department of Agriculture, Bureau of Plant Industry, Girls' Demonstration Work, Washington, January, 1913, pp. 1-2.

[28] For a full statement of the work of the Columbus Schools see "Industrial Education in Columbus,["] Ga., R. B. Daniel, U. S. Bureau of Education, Bulletin 535, Government Printing Office, 1913. Also, The Annual Report of the Columbus Public Schools for the Year Ending August 1, 1913.

[29] Annual report of the Columbus Public Schools, 1913, p. 18.

CHAPTER XIII

THE SPIRIT OF THE NEW EDUCATION

I The Standard of Education

The educational experiments described in the preceding chapters are replete with the spirit of the New Education. From the virile educational systems of the country a protest is being sounded against traditional formalism. School men have learned that that which is is not necessarily right. Each concept, each method, must run the gauntlet of critical analysis. It is not sufficient to allege in support of an educational principle that the results derived from its application have been satisfactory in the past. Insistently the question is repeated, "What are its effects upon the problems of to-day?"

Educational ancestor worship is no more acceptable to the progressive spirit of the Western World than is ancestor worship in any other form. The past has made its contribution, and has died in making it. For the contribution the present is grateful, but it must steadfastly refuse in its own name, and in the name of the future, to be bound by any decree of the past which will not stand the acid test of present experience.

The old education was beset by traditionalism. Under its dominance, education, defined once and for all, was established as a standard to which men must attain; hence a preceptor, guiding his young charges along the straight path to knowledge, might, with perfect confidence, admonish them, "Lo here, the three R's is education," or "Lo there, Greek and higher mathematics is education," according as his training had been in the three R's or in Greek. In either case he felt certain of his general ground. Once and for all the educational standard had been set. By that standard new ideas were judged, and either justified or condemned.

Under this predetermined scheme there was a formula for education—a formula as definite as that for making bread or pickling pork. The formula was applied to each child who presented himself to the administration. If the formula worked successfully the child was declared educated in the same way that pork which has been successfully treated by the proper processes is declared to be pickled. If the formula did not work the child was not educated. He sat in school with a dunce-cap upon his head, or else played hookey and spent his hours in fishing, swimming or idling.

Perhaps, in view of the recent contributions of science, it would be more illuminating to say that the old education inoculated the child with a predetermined educational virus. If the virus "took" the child was declared immune to the bacteria of ignorance, illiteracy, stupidity and other prevalent social complaints. If the virus did not take the schoolmaster ostentatiously washed his hands of the recreant.

II Standardization Was a Failure

Only one argument need be urged against this method of attacking the educational problem—it did not work. In the first place, the most brilliant school successes often turned out to be the most arrant life failures, while the school derelicts frequently became life successes of stellar magnitude. To the thinking man the inference was plain; the formula was not an unqualified success. Not only was this true of the children who went through school, but there were crowds of children for whom the school held no attraction whatever. They attended a few sessions, wasted a scant bit of energy in educational effort, and then dropped out, hopeless of obtaining results by further "study."

The old education read out of the school those children who could not benefit by its teachings. How utterly different the concept which has gripped the minds of progressive, modern educators! Under their guidance education has become what Herbert Spencer called it—a preparation for complete living. No longer a fixed, objective standard, education has been recognized as an enlargement of the life horizon of each individual boy or girl in the community. "Teach us individual needs," proclaim the educational progressives, "and we will tell you what the character of education must be."

Thus has education ceased to be an objective standard, created by one age and handed down rigidly immobile to the ages succeeding. Instead it is accepted as a fulfilment—a complement—to child needs. Always education has been regarded as a process of molding life and character. The chief difference between the old and the new education is that the old education made a mold, and then forced the child to fit the mold, while the new education begins by determining the character of child needs, and then fits the mold to the needs. The old education was like the farmer who built a corn-sheller, and then attempted to find ears of corn which would fit into the sheller; the new education is like the farmer who first measured the corn and then built his sheller to fit the corn. The old education selected the class which was able to conform to its requirements; the new education serves all classes.

III Education as Growth

Under the impetus given to it by modern thinkers, education has become the direction of growth, rather than the application of a formula. The child is a developing creature. It has become the function of education to watch over and guide the development.

Nor do the modern schools consider mental development as the sole object of educational endeavor. Physical growth is an equally essential part of child life. Therefore the direction of physical growth becomes just as vital a part of the educational machinery. Aesthetic and spiritual growth require like emphasis. Each phase of child life receives independent consideration.

The old education through mental impression is giving way before the new education through physical, mental and spiritual expression. Expression is the essence of growth; and since the school is to foster child growth it must place child expression in a place of paramount importance.

Child needs, rather than abstract standards, have thus become the basis of school activity. The old education developed its course of study by surveying the interests of adults, and picking from among them those, apparently the most simple, which were fit for children. The new education applies the laboratory method—studying children and their interests—reports, among its other findings, the quite evident fact that children enter into life as whole-heartedly as adults; that the field of their interest lies, not in the left-over problems of older people, but in their own problems and processes; and that therefore the educator must found his philosophy and his practice on an understanding of the child and child needs.

There is in the world a phenomenon called adult life, with its phases, problems and ideals. There is likewise in the world a phenomenon called child life, with its phases, problems and ideals. A complete understanding of either may not be derived through a study of the other. Child needs exist separate from and different from adult needs. It is the business of the new education to understand them and meet them.

Two appeals are reaching the ears of the modern educator: the first, the appeal of the child; the second, the appeal of the community. The appeal of the child is an appeal for the opportunity of developing all of its faculties. Physically, children grow. The school, recognizing this fact, is making a vigorous effort to break the shell of custom, which has confined its activities to purely intellectual pursuits, and provide a physical training which will lead the school child to perfect normal body growth, as well as normal growth of mind. Even in its intellectual activity the school is recognizing the importance of making the child mind an active machine for thought, rather than a passive storehouse for information. Though less emphasized, the training for sensual growth is becoming of ever increasing importance in the new education. Above all, the aesthetic side of child life is being expanded in an effort to round out a completed adulthood.

IV Child Needs and Community Needs

The recognition of child needs, which forms so integral a part of the new education, is paralleled by a similar recognition of the needs of the community. The progressive educator is laying aside for a moment the details of his task, and asking himself the pertinent question: "What should the community expect in return for the annual expenditure of a billion dollars on public education?" What are community needs if not the needs for manhood and womanhood? They are well summed up in three words—virility, efficiency, citizenship. Possessed of those attributes a group of individuals rounds itself inevitably into a vigorous, progressive community. They are normal qualities which a people must demand if their social standards are to be maintained. Since they constitute so vital an element in social life, a community lavish in its expenditures for schools may surely expect the school product to be virile, efficient, worthy citizens. The new education, recognizing the justice of this demand, is crying out insistently for social, as well as individual, training in the school.

The new educational institutions have set themselves to meet the needs of the child and of the community. Their success depends upon their ability to understand these needs and to supply them.

The old-fashioned schoolmaster asked: "How can I compel?" His answer was the rod. The modern schoolmaster asks: "How can I direct?" His answer is a laboratory, open-minded, scientific method, and a host of varied courses designed to meet the needs of individual children and of individual communities.

Communities vary as greatly in their characteristics as do children. It is now certain that no formula will provide education for all children. Each new study of community needs makes it more evident that no system will supply education for all communities. It is the business of the educator to study the individual child and the individual community, and then to provide an education that will assist both to grow normally and soundly in all of their parts.

V The Final Test of Education

The school is a servant, not a master. In that fact lies its greatness—the greatness of its opportunity and of its responsibility. As an institution its object is service—assistance in growth. Development is the goal of education. Virility, efficiency, citizenship, manhood, womanhood—these are its legitimate products. Its tools and formulas are such as will most effectively serve these ends. When the increase of knowledge leads to new methods and formulas which will prove more effective than the old ones, then the old ones must be laid aside, reverently, perhaps, but none the less firmly, and the new ones adopted. Changes may not be made hastily and without due consideration; but when experiment has shown that the new device is more advantageous in furthering the objects of education than the old and tried formulas, a change is inevitable.

The first and last word on the subject is spoken when this question is asked and answered: "Does education exist for children, or do children exist for education?"

If children exist for education, then it is just that an objective educational standard should be created; it is fair that a hard and fast course of study be mapped out in conformity with that standard; it is right that educational machinery be constructed which automatically turns away from the schools any child who does not conform to the school system as it is. If children exist for education, they should either conform to its requirements, or else, if they will not or cannot conform, they should be mercilessly thrust aside.

If, on the other hand, education exists for children, then the primal consideration must be child needs. If any one child, or any group of children, has needs which are not met by existing educational institutions, then these institutions must be remodeled. If an adequate congenial education is a part of the birthright of every American child, then educational institutions must be reorganized and reshaped until they provide that birthright in the fullest possible measure.

Already the answer has been formulated. Already educators have recognized the potency of the saying: "The schools were made for the children, not the children for the schools." Hence it follows that no school system is so sacred, no method of teaching so venerable, no textbook so infallible, no machinery of administration so permanent, that it must not give way before the educational needs of childhood.

Concerning the educational problem of to-day, yesterday cannot speak with authority. Each age has its problems—problems which may be solved by that age, or handed on unsolved to the future. The past is dead. Only its voice—its advice and suggestion—serves as a guide or as a warning. Of authority it should have not an atom.

The educational opportunities of to-day are without peer. The educational machinery, ready at hand, is being transformed to meet the newly understood needs of the child and of the community. The spirit of the new education is the spirit of service, the spirit of fair dealing, the spirit of growth for the individual and of advancement for society. Here are individual needs. There are aligned the social obligations and requirements of the age. In so far as it lies within the power of the school, the children who leave its doors shall have their needs supplied, and shall be equipped to play their part as virile, efficient citizens in a greater community. Such is the spirit of the new education.

www.ingramcontent.com/pod-product-compliance
Lightning Source LLC
Chambersburg PA
CBHW081109080526
44587CB00021B/3515